THE SUPREME COURT

Ann E. Weiss

ENSLOW PUBLISHERS, INC.

Bloy St. & Ramsey Ave.   P.O. Box 38
Box 777   Aldershot
Hillside, N.J. 07205   Hants GU12 6BP
U.S.A.   U.K.

Library of Congress Cataloging in Publication Data

Weiss, Ann E., 1943-
    The Supreme Court.

    Bibliography: p.
    Includes index.
    Summary: Uses examples from cases to present a history of the Supreme Court and considers the future of the Court.
    1. United states. Supreme Court—History—Juvenile literature. [1. United States. Supreme Court—History] I. Title.
KF8742.Z9W45   1987   347.73'26'09   86-8929
ISBN 0-89490-131-1   347.3073509

Printed in the United States of America

10 9 8 7 6 5 4 3 2

Contents

1

A Case for the Court

"No smoking in school." That is one of the rules at Piscataway High School in Piscataway, New Jersey. It is a rule that could change your life.

How? It all started one day in 1980, when a teacher at Piscataway High accused a girl of smoking in a lavatory. The girl denied it—and ignited a controversy that lasted over four years and ended up in the Supreme Court of the United States. The controversy also affected the legal rights of every student in every public school across the country.

Positive that the girl had broken the no-smoking rule, the Piscataway teacher reported the matter to an assistant vice-principal. The school official ordered the girl to hand over her pocketbook so he could check inside for cigarettes.

He found some. What was more, he spotted a package of cigarette papers. Was the girl using the papers for rolling joints? The suspicious assistant vice-principal rummaged deeper into the bag. There at the bottom was a packet of marijuana. With it were $40 and written notes which showed that the girl had been selling the drug.

Selling a substance like marijuana is against the law, and Piscataway school officials promptly turned the girl over to the police. She was ordered to appear in juvenile court.

In New Jersey, as elsewhere, juvenile court is one of the lowest courts in the state court system. (See chart, page 91.)

Like other low courts, such as police court, family court, divorce court, and small-claims court, juvenile courts have strictly limited jurisdiction. "Jurisdiction" means the legal power to hear and decide cases. It comes from two Latin words, *jus,* meaning "law," and *dictio,* "speaking." As their name suggests, juvenile courts hear only those cases that involve minors—boys and girls under the age of eighteen. The names of defendants in juvenile court cases are not made public, so the Piscataway girl accused of peddling marijuana was referred to only by her initials, T.L.O.

The judge who heard T.L.O.'s case found no reason to question the police evidence against her. T.L.O. was ruled a delinquent and put on probation for a year. She was also ordered expelled from school.

But the girl and her family were determined to fight the expulsion and the delinquency ruling. Through their lawyer, the O.'s charged that the school authorities had acted illegally. The assistant vice-principal had had no right to seize T.L.O.'s pocketbook and search it, they maintained. As a citizen of the United States, T. was protected against "unreasonable searches." People in this country are guaranteed the right to remain "secure in their persons . . . and effects," the family's lawyer pointed out. This guarantee is contained in the U.S. Constitution, the document that lays down the basic rules under which our country is governed. People's rights with regard to "unreasonable searches" are spelled out in the Fourth Amendment to the Constitution.

People have other rights under the Constitution. When a lower court decision goes against them, as it did in T.L.O.'s case, they have the right to ask a higher court to examine that decision. Such a request is called an appeal, and the court to which it is made is called an appellate court. In New Jersey, the highest appellate court in the state court system is the state supreme court. Every state has a similar high court, although some have different names for it—supreme court of errors, court of appeals, supreme judicial court, and so on.

The O.'s took their appeal to the New Jersey Supreme Court, and in 1983, the judges on that court made their decision. The O.'s were correct, the judges said. The school official had acted illegally. He had ignored the constitutional rule forbidding unreasonable searches. If he had followed the rule, he would not have examined T.'s pocketbook. If he had not examined it, he would not have found the marijuana, the money, and the notes. Without that evidence, the police would have had no case. T.L.O. would never have had to appear in court or been judged delinquent, put on probation, or ordered expelled.

Since T.'s constitutional rights had been violated, the New Jersey Supreme Court went on, her conviction was in error. It must be "reversed." T. was no longer to be considered a delinquent, and the expulsion order must be lifted.

The state supreme court decision did not mark the end of T.'s case, though. Private citizens are not the only ones who are allowed to appeal unfavorable court decisions. Prosecutors, the lawyers who present the government's case against the accused in court, may also appeal if they think the court has made a mistake. The New Jersey prosecutors who worked on T.'s case thought just that. They believed that schoolchildren are not protected by the Fourth Amendment in the same way adults are. So the prosecutors appealed to an even higher court to hear the evidence once more. The only court higher than a state supreme court is the United States Supreme Court.

To the satisfaction of the New Jersey prosecutors, the justices of the U.S. Supreme Court agreed to consider the case of *New Jersey* v. *T.L.O.* (The "v." stands for *versus,* Latin for "against.") If they had not agreed, the New Jersey Supreme Court decision in favor of T.L.O. would have stood as final. As it was, the prosecutors now had one last chance to win. The U.S. Supreme Court is the highest court in the land, at the top of the federal court system as well as above each state supreme court. (See chart, page 90.) U.S. Supreme Court decisions are final; there is no higher court to which a case can be appealed. Whichever side won in the Supreme Court— New Jersey or T.L.O.—would win for good.

In March 1984, state prosecutors and T.L.O.'s lawyers traveled to Washington, D.C., where the Supreme Court sits. The white marble court building is opposite the U.S. Capitol building and next to the Library of Congress. Huge pillars support its porch roof. Above the pillars is carved the Court's motto: Equal Justice Under Law.

At the heart of the Supreme Court building is the courtroom in which public sessions are held. It is an impressive room, its walls lined with twenty-four marble columns. At the back of the room are seats for spectators—people who have an interest in a particular case or those who are curious about the Supreme Court in general. The nine Supreme Court justices sit at the front of the room in high-backed chairs behind a gently curving mahogany bench. The Chief Justice, the head of the Court, sits in the middle, with four associate justices on either side. Between the justices' bench and the spectators' seats is space for the lawyers who argue cases. It was in this part of the room that the prosecutors and defense lawyers in *New Jersey* v. *T.L.O.* rose to present their evidence.

That evidence was massive, as it almost always is in Supreme Court cases. First, there was the entire record of the case—the papers associated with it. These papers included typed transcripts of all the evidence given in various courts since 1980, as well as the opinions of the judges who had handed down decisions along the way.

In addition, prosecutors and defense attorneys presented briefs—written arguments that stated the facts of the case as each side saw them. The brief presented by T.L.O.'s lawyers dealt largely with what they believed to be the girl's legal rights under the Fourth Amendment. The brief filed by the prosecutors dwelt on the responsibility of school authorities to keep order and to compel students to obey the rules. It stressed the opinion that the Fourth Amendment protects people only against "unreasonable" searches by the police and other law enforcement officials. The amendment does not apply at all in school situations, the New Jersey brief stated.

The lawyers repeated these opposing points of view when the justices called upon them to argue the case orally. Oral arguments are part of many important Supreme Court cases. As the lawyers for each side speak, the justices may interrupt, asking questions and even offering arguments, in order to understand as fully as possible the exact legal points being made.

Usually, each side gets thirty minutes for oral argument, although the justices may make more time available if they think it is needed. In the case of *New Jersey* v. *T.L.O.*, the justices did decide that more time was necessary. They asked the lawyers to come back to reargue the case the following October.

After hearing the second round of arguments, the justices met privately, in conference, to discuss the case. They reviewed the oral presentations, the briefs, the previous testimony, and the verdicts. At last they were ready to come to a decision.

In arriving at that decision, the justices followed a procedure that has become traditional over the years. The Chief Justice speaks first, outlining the case in general terms and suggesting how it might be resolved, but not expressing a firm opinion one way or the other. Next, the justices discuss the case, debating the issues involved and considering the views of each member of the Court. Then each associate justice explains how he or she is voting and why. The associates speak in turn, starting with the one who has been on the Court the shortest length of time and ending with the one who is most senior. Last of all, the Chief Justice votes.

Supreme Court decisions are determined by a simple majority. Sometimes the decision is unanimous, with all nine justices voting the same way. Sometimes it is very close, 5–4. In *New Jersey* v. *T.L.O.*, the vote was 6–3. Three justices agreed with T. that the Fourth Amendment did protect her against the kind of search the assistant vice-principal had conducted. Six, including the Chief Justice, believed that the Fourth Amendment protects students in some situations but not in all. In their view, school officials have some of the same rights over children that parents have. It would not be unreasonable for parents to search a fourteen-year-old daughter's belongings if they suspected her of wrongdoing. Therefore, the six agreed, it is reasonable—and legal—for school authorities to do the same.

The Supreme Court decision reversed the finding of the New Jersey Supreme Court. Once more, T.L.O. was judged to have been guilty of selling marijuana. The expulsion order, however, was not renewed. As a matter of fact, it had never been enforced. T.L.O. was allowed to continue going to school while her case was in the courts. She graduated from high school in 1984.

As soon as the Court made its decision, the Chief Justice assigned one of the five associate justices who had voted with the majority to write the "majority opinion." In preparing this opinion, the justice took care to mention each of the points that had led the Court to decide the case as it had. The idea that schools may sometimes act *in loco parentis* ("in place of parents"), the fact that many schools have become violent places where crime needs to be controlled, and the belief that the Piscataway school official's search was not unreasonable under the circumstances all appear in the majority decision.

This opinion is important, and not just to the parties in *New Jersey* v. *T.L.O.* Like all Supreme Court decisions, *New Jersey* v. *T.L.O.* is binding, not merely upon T.L.O., Piscataway High, the New Jersey Supreme Court, and the state itself, but also upon courts, school students, and school officials in all fifty states. As of January 15, 1985, the day the decision was announced, public school students could no longer claim that the Fourth Amendment protected them from being searched by school authorities on school property. Unless the Supreme Court changes its mind, a search need only be "reasonable" to be legal.

That was a point that bothered the three associate justices who had voted in the minority. Two of the three wrote dissenting opinions, in which they explained why they disagreed with the majority. The "reasonableness" standard set up by the majority was "unclear,"one declared. What seems reasonable to one person may not seem reasonable to another.

The other dissenters agreed. In a separate dissenting opinion, one wrote, "For the Court, a search for curlers and sunglasses in order to enforce the school dress code is apparently just as important as a search for evidence of heroin addiction or violent gang activity." A wiser course, he went on, would have been for the Court to permit searches only when school authorities "have reason to believe that the search will uncover *evidence that the student is violating the law or engaging in conduct that is seriously disruptive.*"

What will happen as a result of the decision in *New Jersey* v. *T.L.O.*? Will public school authorities begin trampling over students' constitutional rights in a rush to search for "curlers and sunglasses"? Or will the authorities find themselves able to impose needed discipline in school classrooms and corridors without seriously threatening anyone's liberties? How will *New Jersey* v. *T.L.O.* affect your school and you?

How will other Supreme Court decisions affect your life? During its 1984 term, which ran from the first Monday in October to July 2, 1985, the Court ruled that public school teachers and officials may not require students to take part in silent prayer. In another case that concerned the relationship between government and religion, the justices said that public money may not be spent to provide remedial education for boys and girls in church-run schools. Other matters considered by the Court during its 1984 term included libel laws, political campaign spending, death penalty laws, and the rights of striking workers.

Supreme Court decisions of the past influence our everyday lives as well. Because of Supreme Court rulings, blacks and whites work and study together in the United States. Because of the Supreme Court, women may obtain legal abortions in this country, workers are free to join labor unions, and the police must respect certain constitutional rights of those they arrest and accuse of committing a crime. Americans' rights to freedom of religion, freedom of speech, and freedom of the press have been protected by Supreme Court decisions. The Supreme Court has declared state laws and even acts of the U.S. Congress to be illegal. It has forced presidents to submit to its will.

How did the Court come to have so much power? Who gave it the right to make such far-reaching decisions? Just what is the Supreme Court?

2

The Supreme Court Is Born

On February 3, 1783, the Treaty of Paris was signed. That treaty marked the end of the American Revolution. Now the United States was officially independent. No longer would its people have to obey the harsh laws passed by England's Parliament. No longer must they honor King George III as their sovereign. From now on, Americans would rule themselves.

At first, they ruled rather badly. The new country's central government was organized under an agreement called the Articles of Confederation. The articles established Congress as the national governing body. But Congress was weak, too weak to compel the thirteen states to act as parts of one larger nation. Each state behaved as if it were a separate country.

In 1787, for instance, New York laid a tax on New Jersey and Connecticut ships that sailed into or out of New York waters. New Jersey reacted by slapping a tax of its own on a New York lighthouse. States had their own armed militias and even printed their own paper money. Confusion grew.

So in May 1787, representatives from twelve states— every one except Rhode Island—met in Philadelphia. At the outset, their aim was simply to strengthen the Articles of Confederation, but almost at once they agreed it was hopeless even to try. Instead, they made up their minds to begin at the beginning and devise a whole new plan of government.

Over the next four months, the fifty-five delegates debated, discussed, argued, and compromised—above all, they compromised. The Constitution they completed on September 17 is a masterpiece of bargaining and conciliation. To begin with, it calls for a single national government, to be divided into three separate branches.

First is the legislative, or lawmaking, branch. Article 1 of the Constitution provides for a strong national Congress. This Congress consists of two houses, the Senate and the House of Representatives. In the Senate, states are represented equally. Each has two senators. Representation in the House is based on population. The more people a state has, the more representatives it elects.

The Constitution's second article created the executive branch of government. It allows for one national leader, a chief executive or president. Article 3 concerns the third branch, the judicial branch. It directed Congress to set up a system of courts of law with "one Supreme Court" at the top.

The kind of government outlined in the Constitution is called a federal government. Unlike the Articles of Confederation, the Constitution concentrates a great deal of power in the hands of a few federal, or national, leaders. It makes the federal government more important than any individual state government.

That fact worried a number of the men at the Constitutional Convention. They thought the new federal government might eventually become powerful enough to threaten the rights of the states. Remembering the English Parliament, they wondered whether Congress would impose unbearable federal taxes. Recalling George III, they asked whether a president might not try to become king—"make one push for the American throne," as a critic from Virginia put it. Such concerns led the delegates to construct a Constitution with built-in safeguards against federal tyranny.

Those safeguards are known as checks and balances. In a series of compromises, the men who framed the Constitution made sure that every power given to one branch of the federal government was matched by powers allotted to the other two. Overall, the three branches check each other. The balance is such that none can seize absolute power.

The president, for example, may ask Congress to pass a particular law. But he cannot force Congress to do so. On the other hand, Congress may enact legislation that the president does not like. In that case, he may veto the legislation—refuse to sign it into law. However, the president cannot block Congress altogether. If he vetoes a piece of legislation, Congress may decide to consider it again. If two-thirds of the members of each house vote in its favor, it becomes law anyway.

The judicial branch is also part of the system of checks and balances. One way the president exerts authority over the judiciary is through his power to appoint federal judges, including Supreme Court justices. One way Congress does the same is through the Senate's right to approve or disapprove those appointments. Senate confirmation of Supreme Court appointments also serves as a congressional check on presidential power. Twenty-six times in our nation's history the Senate has failed to approve a president's choice for a Supreme Court seat.

Another congressional check on the president and the judiciary lies in the power of impeachment. Impeachment is the process by which a president, Supreme Court justice, or other officer of the U.S. government may be removed from office. Under the Constitution, the House may vote to impeach an official it believes guilty of misconduct. Then that official goes on trial in the Senate. If two-thirds of the senators vote for conviction, the official must step down. Only one Supreme Court justice has ever been impeached, and in that case, the Senate did not vote to remove him.

The Supreme Court has powers of its own to balance the powers of Congress and the president. It is through the judiciary that those accused of breaking the law are tried and, if found guilty, punished. Even the president is subject to the power of the judicial branch. And it is the Chief Justice who presides over the trial of an impeached president.

Other checks and balances were written into the Constitution during that summer of 1787. We will see them in action throughout this book. But of all the Supreme Court's powers to curb the might of the other two branches of government, the most vital one was never mentioned directly in Article 3 or anywhere else. We will see more about that later, too.

Once the Constitution was complete, copies of it were sent to each state legislature. Nine of the thirteen would have to ratify it—agree to it—before it could go into effect.

Ratification was not certain in the fall of 1787. Legislators in several states had serious doubts about the Constitution. Some thought it did not say enough about protecting citizens' individual civil liberties—their basic rights to freedom of speech and religion, to trial by jury, and so forth. These men were reluctant to ratify unless a "bill of rights" was added. Others were concerned because they thought the Constitution gave too much authority to the federal government and not enough to the states. They wanted to add an amendment to protect the right of each state to handle its own affairs without interference from national leaders.

Throughout the rest of 1787 and into 1788, arguments for and against the Constitution raged up and down the Atlantic seaboard. Those in favor of ratification called themselves federalists. They included men like George Washington and John Adams. Opponents were called antifederalists. Revolutionary War patriot Patrick Henry of Virginia was among them.

By June 1788 the arguing was over. Nine state legislatures had ratified the Constitution. In return, it was agreed that Congress would propose a bill of rights as soon as possible.

The Bill of Rights became part of the Constitution three years later. Of its ten amendments, nine list rights of the people. The tenth is a states' rights amendment. It reserves for the states "powers not delegated to the United States by the Constitution."

March 4, 1789, was the date chosen for the new government to take office, although it was not until the end of April that President George Washington was inaugurated and Congress began work. One of the legislators' first jobs, as set forth in Article 3 of the Constitution, was to establish a system of courts. In September, Congress fulfilled its responsibility by passing the Judiciary Act of 1789. The president signed it into law. Much of this law remains in force today.

The 1789 law, like the Constitution itself, represents a compromise. Those members of Congress who favored states' rights over federal rights saw to it that lower federal courts were located around the country, not concentrated in the federal capital. The act set up a total of thirteen federal district courts. (As the country has grown, so has the number of such courts. Today there are ninety-four.) The states' righters also made sure the federal court system would not put an end to the separate state courts. As we saw in Chapter 1, state and federal courts exist side by side in the United States.

At the same time, congressmen who supported the strongest possible federal government insisted upon granting broad powers to the Supreme Court. One of those powers was laid down in Section 25 of the Judiciary Act. That section gave the Court the right to consider cases that involve a conflict between state power and federal power. Under it, the Court may review decisions in which a state supreme court has said that a state law is legally binding upon the people of that state. Section 25 also permits Court review when a state supreme court rules that citizens of that state do not have to obey a federal law.

Section 25 made the Supreme Court truly supreme. Thanks to it, no state legislature, nor any state court, could put itself above the Supreme Court. In all legal controversies between state and federal authority, the highest justices in the federal judiciary would have the last word.

The Judiciary Act of 1789 also set Supreme Court membership at six—one Chief Justice and five associates. Congress's power to fix the Court's size is another way the legislative branch checks and balances the judicial. Several times over the years, Congress has availed itself of this power and has voted to raise or lower the number of justices on the Court.

The Judiciary Act also created three federal circuit courts of appeal. Each covered a separate part of the country. (Today the circuit courts number thirteen.) Back in 1789, each circuit court was composed of two Supreme Court justices and one federal district judge from that circuit. Circuit court judges had to travel throughout the area they covered in order to hear appellate cases. Requiring Supreme Court justices to spend part of the year "riding the circuit" over rough roads and wilderness trails was yet another way that Congress sought to keep them from exercising too much authority in the nation's capital.

Once Congress finished organizing the federal judiciary, it was up to the president to make his appointments. An ardent federalist, President Washington was careful to choose judges who were equally committed to the idea of a strong federal government. In all, during his eight years in office, Washington made eleven nominations to the Supreme Court. He named three Chief Justices: John Jay, John Rutledge, and Oliver Ellsworth. Rutledge was rejected by the Senate. (A complete list of Supreme Court justices appears on page 92.)

The first Supreme Court terms were not busy. The justices rode their circuits, hearing appeals and deciding cases. But few cases came to them when they sat in the federal capital— first New York City, then Philadelphia, and finally, after 1800, Washington, D.C. During its first twelve years, the Court considered only sixty cases. About a third concerned America's relations with other nations or shipping and other maritime affairs. Article 3 assigns such cases to the Supreme Court.

Article 3 also charges the Court with hearing cases involving U.S. laws and treaties, cases that concern ambassadors and other representatives to foreign lands, and controversies between states and between citizens of different states. When an ambassador or a state is involved, the Supreme Court has original jurisdiction. That means it is the first and only court to hear the case.

In other matters, the Court has appellate jurisdiction—it hears appeals of lower state or federal court decisions. However, as Article 3 makes clear, Congress has the right to limit Supreme Court jurisdiction. If it wishes, Congress can simply deny the Court the right to hear a certain type of case. If it does, the justices must obey the law. This is still another congressional check on judicial power.

Congress has other ways to express its displeasure with the Court. One is to pass a law or to propose a constitutional amendment designated to "get around" a particular ruling. Congress did this for the first time in 1794.

The ruling that led to the Eleventh Amendment came in the case of *Chisholm* v. *Georgia.* It involved a sum of money owed by the state of Georgia to a South Carolina man. *Chisholm* reached the Supreme Court in 1792. Two years later, the justices decided that Georgia must pay its debt.

States' righters reacted furiously. How dare the justices tell a state how to conduct its affairs! Georgia legislators debated a bill that would have made it a crime to enforce the ruling. Punishment for committing that crime would have been hanging "without benefit of clergy." In Congress, an Eleventh Amendment was quickly approved and ratified by the states. This amendment took away the Supreme Court's rights to consider cases in which a citizen of one state seeks to sue another state. For the first time, Congress had acted to thwart the Court.

Aside from the *Chisholm* controversy, however, relations among the three branches of government were peaceful during the nation's first years. That was largely because most people in the federal government had the same ideas about what was good for America and how the country ought to be run. As federalists, they believed in strong central government. Moreover, just about all of the nation's earliest leaders were the same kind of people from the same kind of background. Virtually without exception, they were well educated and well-to-do. Not surprisingly, they were convinced that the best government was one led by well-educated men acting to protect wealth and property.

Yet not everyone in the country was sympathetic to that way of thinking. Many Americans were small farmers, artisans, and traders who were not rich at all. The number of such Americans was growing in the 1790s as more and more European immigrants arrived in the United States. New states were joining the original thirteen, too—states like Kentucky and Tennessee, most of whose people were hardy, self-reliant pioneers. When these people voted for members of Congress, they cast their ballots for men who believed that government should act on behalf of all citizens, not just those with money.

Before long, Congress began to change. Wealthy conservative federalists were still in the majority. But a growing number of congressmen had "republican" or "democratic" ideas. They did not believe in government by and for the wealthy and educated, but in government by and for all the people.

By the mid-1790s, disagreements between federalists and "democratic-republicans" had produced two separate and distinct political groups. The leader of the Democratic-Republican party was Thomas Jefferson. The Federalist party's leader was John Adams, who had served eight years as Washington's vice-president. In 1796, Adams was elected president.

The new chief executive and his Federalist supporters in Congress could see that their political strength was weakening while Democratic-Republican ideas were becoming more and more popular. They therefore enacted laws to make it harder for the new party to win supporters and elect candidates to office. The laws were known as the Alien and Sedition Acts.

In passing them, the president and Congress seemed to have forgotten all about the First Amendment. Under the Alien and Sedition Acts, Americans lost the right to speak and write freely. Anyone who said anything against the president or the federal government, or even against the Federalist party, might be thrown in jail. Federal judges did not hesitate to mete out stiff sentences to those convicted of breaking the new laws. The judges, after all, were Federalists themselves.

Not even the Alien and Sedition Acts could stop the spread of Democratic-Republicanism, however. In the election of 1800, Americans chose Thomas Jefferson as president. Members of the new party won a majority in the House and gained strength in the Senate. The Federalists' day seemed to be ending.

But Federalist leaders had a plan for hanging on to power. The election was over, but Adams and the Federalist Congress would not leave office until March 4, 1801. Before then, they would act to tighten their grip on the judicial branch. With this in mind, the outgoing Federalists in Congress passed a new Judiciary Act.

The Judiciary Act of 1801 included some needed reforms. It said that Supreme Court justices need not ride the circuits any more, for example. But it also created a number of new federal judgeships. The plan was for President Adams to "pack" the judiciary full of loyal Federalists before March 4.

Adams did his best, but time was short. Although the president signed numerous commissions appointing Federalist judges, several of the commissions still had not been delivered by midnight of March 3, the hour at which Adams's term ran out. When Jefferson was sworn in as president, these commissions remained in the office of Adams's secretary of state. President Jefferson told *his* secretary of state, James Madison, to hold on to them. Madison did.

Among the undelivered commissions was one appointing a man named William Marbury as a justice of the peace for the District of Columbia. Marbury, eager to assume office, brought suit against Madison. He asked the Supreme Court to order the secretary of state to deliver his commission. The Judiciary Act of 1789 gave the Court the right to issue such an order, Marbury pointed out.

At this time, the Chief Justice was John Marshall. A Federalist, Marshall had been appointed to the Court by Adams just weeks before. Speaking for the Court, Marshall ordered Madison to "show cause" why he should not deliver Marbury's commission. It looked as though Marshall was going to insist upon getting Adams's last-minute appointees, the "midnight judges," onto federal court benches. If he did, the Federalists' plan would succeed. The judiciary would remain in their hands.

The Democratic-Republicans who now controlled Congress were determined to keep that from happening. They repealed the Judiciary Act of 1801, "uncreating" the new federal judgeships. The repeal meant that the Supreme Court justices must resume circuit riding. Congress also forbade the Court to meet again for fourteen months.

Congress had won—or so it seemed. The legislative branch had checked the judicial. Marshall and the other justices went meekly back to their circuits.

They also went along with the order to suspend their sessions. The Court did not meet at all in 1802. When the justices did gather once more, in February 1803, *Marbury* v. *Madison* was right there on the docket—the list of cases waiting to be heard.

It was Chief Justice Marshall who wrote the majority opinion in *Marbury* v. *Madison*. That opinion came in two parts. First, Marshall ruled that Marbury had every right to receive his commission. But, he went on, the Court had no power to force Madison to deliver it. The Judiciary Act of 1789 gave the Court that power, true. But nowhere in the Constitution is it written that that power is Congress's to give. Article 3 allows Congress to limit the Court's jurisdiction but says nothing about enlarging it. In authorizing the Supreme Court to issue orders like the one Marbury was demanding, Congress had overstepped its legal authority. It had not followed the Constitution. Congress, Marshall concluded, had acted *un*constitutionally.

Everyone won something in *Marbury* v. *Madison*—except Marbury himself. Jefferson got to appoint judges of his own political party. Congress had the satisfaction of knowing that more Democratic-Republicans would be added to the federal judiciary in the future.

But the Supreme Court won the greatest victory. Led by Chief Justice Marshall, the Court had declared its right to decide when a law is constitutional and when it is not. "It is emphatically the province and duty of the judicial department to say what the law is," Marshall wrote. No one disputed him. With those words, the Court assumed the right of judicial review—the right to rule on the constitutionality of actions taken by Congress, the president, and the states.

Marbury v. *Madison* established the Constitution as the supreme law of the land. Not even president and Congress together can override it. The right to judicial review is the

Supreme Court's most vital check on the other branches of government—a check that is nowhere explicitly mentioned in the Constitution.

Now that it had won that right, the Court was ready to undertake a leading role in the shaping of the nation.

Chief Justices

John Jay	1790-1795
†John Rutledge	1795
Oliver Ellsworth	1796-1800
John Marshall	1801-1835

Associate Justices

James Wilson	1789-1798
John Rutledge	1790-1791
William Cushing	1790-1810
John Blair	1790-1796
James Iredell	1790-1799
Thomas Johnson	1792-1793
William Paterson	1793-1806
Samuel Chase	1796-1811
Bushrod Washington	1799-1829
Alfred Moore	1800-1804

†appointment not confirmed by Senate

3

The Marshall Court

John Marshall served as Chief Justice of the United States for thirty-four years. During that time, from 1801 to 1835, the Supreme Court underwent enormous changes.

The most fundamental, of course, came when the justices announced their decision in *Marbury* v. *Madison*. Assuming the right to judicial review transformed the Court into a major force in the life of the nation. Only after 1803 was the judiciary truly equal to the other two branches of the federal government.

Other changes came to the Supreme Court during Marshall's years there. Its size varied. Membership had started at six in 1789. Then Congress reduced it to five in 1801. In 1807, it jumped to seven.

As time passed, the justices had more work to do. Up until 1801, they heard an average of five cases a year. Between then and 1835, they heard 1215 cases, more than thirty-five yearly.

As the justices' work increased, so did their salaries. In 1789, the Chief Justice was paid $4000 annually. Associate justices received $3500. By 1819, the Chief Justice was getting $5000; associates, $4500.

Housing for the Supreme Court also improved with time. On the day President Adams appointed Marshall as Chief Justice, the commissioners of the new capital city of Washington,

D.C., dispatched a worried note to Congress. "As no house has been provided for the Judiciary," the commissioners wrote, "we hope the Supreme Court may be accommodated with a room in the Capitol." Congress cooperated, even though its own quarters were hardly in a finished state in 1801. The justices were offered the use of a small room in a basement under the north end of the Capitol. It was here that the court reached its decision in *Marbury*. Later, the room became part of the Senate barbershop.

In 1808, the Court moved into another part of the Capitol, the not-yet-completed wing that was eventually to lodge the House of Representatives. The justices found their new meeting place "so inconvenient and cold" that they rented a room in a nearby tavern and held sessions there. Two years later, as the Capitol neared completion, the Court moved back in. It was to continue meeting there for a century and a quarter.

Other Court changes during the first third of the nineteenth century were more profound. They went far beyond such mundane matters as housing and salaries. These changes had to do with the way the Court regarded itself and its duties, and most of them grew out of the character and personality of one man, Chief Justice John Marshall.

Marshall is considered one of the greatest Chief Justices— perhaps *the* greatest Chief Justice—ever to sit on the bench. He stayed there longer than any other Chief Justice before or since, and he was an exceptionally forceful leader. Throughout most of his tenure, Marshall dominated the Court. In case after case, he managed to persuade the other justices to agree with his opinions and to make decisions that reflected his beliefs and convictions.

Those convictions were staunchly Federalist. Like the Federalist president who had appointed him, Marshall believed in a strong national government. In any conflict between state rights and federal rights, he almost automatically came down on the federal side. Marshall was also committed to the idea that it is government's responsibility to protect wealth and property and to encourage private business to expand and grow. In this, too, he reflected Federalist philosophy.

It was Marshall's Federalism that lay behind his opinion in *Marbury* v. *Madison*. In that case, as we saw, he held that the Court had no authority to issue an order for Secretary of State Madison to deliver William Marbury's justice-of-the-peace commission. When Congress gave the Court that power in 1789, Marshall ruled, it had acted unconstitutionally.

Actually, as historians have pointed out, Marshall could have found differently in the case. A slightly altered interpretation of the wording of the law would have permitted him to send Marbury back to a district court to get his order. But the Chief Justice did not choose to interpret the law that way. Why not?

Because John Marshall saw in *Marbury* a chance to demonstrate, once and for all, that the federal Constitution is the ultimate source of governmental authority in the United States. As a Federalist, he grasped the opportunity to make it absolutely clear that the Constitution stands above any act of Congress, any presidential order, or any claim to states' rights. To prove the point, Marshall was willing to sacrifice Marbury's commission. Federalism would be better served by pronouncing the authority of the Constitution and the Court's right to judicial review than by adding a few more Federalists to the nation's courts, Marshall thought.

The way in which Marshall approached the issues in *Marbury* showed him to be a "judicial activist." An activist justice is one who looks at cases and the Constitution broadly, using them to challenge and enlarge the scope of the law. That was what Marshall did when he turned the routine *Marbury* case into a means of assuming the right to judicial review.

To his satisfaction, Marshall got the Court to vote unanimously in *Marbury*. Chief Justices like a decision to be unanimous, especially in important or controversial cases. They know that if the justices stand united on an issue it makes their decision look firmer and more authoritative.

Getting a unanimous decision in *Marbury* was not so difficult. In 1803, the Supreme Court was still made up entirely of Federalists. Soon that was to change. In 1804, Thomas Jefferson made his first Court appointment, and before his second term expired in 1809, the Democratic-Republican president had named two other associate justices. Three years later, in 1812, the Court's political balance shifted for good. Republicans (as they were beginning to be called, although they were not related to our present-day Republican party) now outnumbered Federalists.

Yet even outnumbered, Marshall dominated Supreme Court thinking. A Republican majority did not keep the Court from handing down decision after decision that strengthened the federal system and permitted that system to encourage business and private enterprise. Three of the most significant of these Marshall Court decisions were *Dartmouth College* v. *Woodward, McCulloch* v. *Maryland,* and *Gibbons* v. *Ogden.*

The first two were decided in 1819. The Dartmouth case involved the New Hampshire college. Dartmouth had been founded in 1769 under a charter issued by what was then the British colony of New Hampshire. Now, the state of New Hampshire had enacted a law to amend the charter and take control of the college. Dartmouth's treasurer, the "Woodward" in the case, sided with the state and tried to enforce its law. But other college officials resisted. They ended by taking Woodward to court.

Woodward won his case in the New Hampshire Supreme Court, which declared the state law valid. Under Section 25 of the Judiciary Act of 1789, that ruling sent the case to the U.S. Supreme Court.

Daniel Webster, the New Hampshire–born lawyer, orator, and statesman, pleaded the school's case orally before the Court. Webster argued that Dartmouth had a chartered right to remain free of state control. A charter is a private business contract, he maintained, that can not be broken by a state legislature.

Marshall agreed. The law was overturned, and Dartmouth stayed independent. The decision was a blow to states' rights. But it encouraged businessmen, who had a strong interest in protecting the validity of contracts.

Businessmen were similarly encouraged by the decision in *McCulloch* v. *Maryland.* At issue here was the second Bank of the United States and the right of a state to tax a branch of that bank.

The second bank had been set up by Congress in 1816. Like the first Bank of the United States, which lasted from 1791 to 1811, this bank was created to lend money to businesses. Naturally, it was popular with wealthy businessmen. But it was unpopular with the nation's less well-to-do, such as its thousands of farmers. In concentrating on big business, farmers claimed, the bank ignored their needs, making it harder than ever for them to earn a decent living.

It was with this in mind that the state of Maryland attempted to tax the Baltimore branch of the bank. A tax bill was prepared and sent to the bank's local cashier, a man named McCulloch. McCulloch refused to pay and went to court. When the Maryland Supreme Court upheld the state's tax law, Section 25 of the Judiciary Act of 1789 was again invoked. The case went to the Supreme Court of the United States.

In considering *McCulloch* v. *Maryland,* the justices had to take into account more than the question of Maryland's tax. Behind that question was another: Should Congress have established the Bank of the United States to begin with? Nowhere does the Constitution give Congress any such right.

Marshall had to concede that the Constitution does not refer to a bank. But after reading and hearing arguments in the case, he could not agree that that omission made the bank unconstitutional. To be sure, Congress did not have an explicit, clearly defined right to set up a bank. But it did have the implied right to do so.

The doctrine of "implied powers" was one of the most important to come from the Marshall Court. It was a prime example of Marshall's spirit of judicial activism. And it added tremendously to the authority of the legislative branch of government.

The Chief Justice based the doctrine on a few words in Section 8 of Article 1 of the Constitution. Congress, says this section, may "make all laws which shall be necessary and proper." In Marshall's view, a national bank was both necessary and proper if American business was to flourish. Thus, Congress had been within its rights in creating the bank.

Moreover, Marshall continued, the implied powers of Congress extend beyond the right to establish a national bank. Congress has the implied right to take any number of actions not specifically mentioned in the Constitution. "Let the end be legitimate, let it be within the scope of the Constitution," he wrote, "and all means which are appropriate . . . are constitutional."

Having found the bank necessary and proper—and therefore constitutional—Marshall declared Maryland's tax unconstitutional. "The power to tax involves the power to destroy," he stated. He meant that, in theory, Maryland could tax the Baltimore branch of the bank into bankruptcy. Any state could tax any federal institution located within its boundaries into extinction. That must not be permitted to happen, the Chief Justice concluded. No state may destroy the work of the federal government or try to get out of obeying its laws— provided those laws meet the Supreme Court's standard of constitutionality.

Five years later, in 1824, the Court again confirmed federal rights over the rights of the states. *Gibbons* v. *Ogden* was a complicated case involving two rival steamboat lines. It grew out of an argument about a New York law that forbade steamboats owned and operated by out-of-staters to enter its waters. The Court decided that New York had no right to enforce such a law. Again, Marshall found the authority for his decision in Section 8 of Article 1, which gives Congress the power "to regulate commerce . . . among the several States." Those words, Marshall reasoned, must mean that the men who wrote the Constitution intended the federal government to make the rules for trade between the states. States might regulate their own trade, but they must not interfere with the trade or business of another state. Marshall's conclusion that the federal government has authority over interstate commerce was to have great significance in the years to come.

To us, looking back from the late twentieth century, decisions like the ones in *Gibbons, McCulloch, Dartmouth,* and *Marbury* may seem to have been inevitable. We take it for granted that the United States is one single nation and not fifty semi-independent ones, that the federal government is supreme, that Congress may take actions not specifically referred to in the Constitution, and that the Supreme Court may judge state and federal laws and weigh them against the Constitution. But in the early nineteenth century, such ideas were only beginning to be commonly accepted. They did not seem inevitable at all. What seemed, and was, inevitable was that the Supreme Court's activism would lead it into clashes with the other branches of government.

One clash came in January 1804, when President Thomas Jefferson asked the House of Representatives to look into the possibility of impeaching Associate Justice Samuel Chase. Chase was a fiercely opinionated Federalist. On at least one occasion, he had spoken out publicly against Jefferson's Republican policies. After a two-month investigation, the House did impeach Chase. His trial before the Senate began in January 1805, with Vice-President Aaron Burr presiding.

It was a dramatic trial and a great political contest. Insults abounded, both inside and outside the Senate chamber. Jefferson described Chase's defense lawyer as an "unprincipled and impudent federal bull-dog." The lawyer responded with liberal use of his favorite curse, "as great a scoundrel as Thomas Jefferson."

In the end, Chase was acquitted. His Republican opponents had needed the votes of two-thirds of the members of the Senate to convict, and they could not get that many. Chase remained on the Court until his death six years later.

Disappointed by their failure to win the support of two-thirds of the Senate, Chase's enemies in Congress introduced a constitutional amendment that would have required only a simple majority for a guilty verdict in an impeachment trial.

Despite the support of President Jefferson, the proposed amendment was defeated that year and the next, and again in 1811 and 1816.

But the battle between the branches of government was not over, and Jefferson continued to help lead the anti-Court forces. In 1821, the former president wrote: "It has long . . . been my opinion . . . that the germ of dissolution of our . . . government is . . . the federal judiciary; an irresponsible body . . . working like gravity by night and by day . . . advancing its noiseless step like a thief . . . until all shall be usurped from the States."

Like others concerned for the rights of the states, Jefferson was convinced that the Court's federalism reflected the ideas of only a minority of rich and powerful Americans. The justices were ignoring the wishes of most ordinary citizens, he thought. To make them more responsive to the majority, Jefferson suggested limiting their terms on the Court. Only if their decisions were popular would their appointments be renewed by the president and reconfirmed by the Senate.

Others advocated even more radical measures to limit Supreme Court power. In December 1821, Senator Richard M. Johnson of Kentucky offered a constitutional amendment to take away the court's right to review the constitutionality of state laws. The amendment would have given that right to the Senate.

Two years later, Johnson came up with another idea— requiring the agreement of two-thirds of the members of the Supreme Court to overturn a state law. As it was, a law could be declared unconstitutional by a simple 4–3 majority. In fact, as the senator pointed out, the majority often consisted of only three because justices were frequently absent during a vote. A third Johnson suggestion was to raise the number of justices from seven to ten. That would give Republican President James Monroe the chance to appoint three new members. It would give the Senate the chance to reject any who were not firm states' righters.

Still another proposal was to repeal Section 25 of the Judiciary Act of 1789. This is the part of the law that gives the Court the right to review state court decisions in which the constitutionality of a state law was upheld, or in which a federal law was declared unconstitutional. Section 25 is what makes the federal Supreme Court the nation's final legal authority.

Of all the Court-curbing ideas around, the one to repeal Section 25 struck the Court and its supporters as the most dangerous—and the one the most likely to pass. A discouraged John Marshall told Associate Justice Joseph Story that it required "no prophet" to predict that Section 25 would be repealed. "The crisis of our Constitution is upon us," Marshall wrote. Story concurred. "If the Twenty-Fifth Section is repealed," he mourned, "the Constitution is practically gone . . . our friends look with great gloom to the future."

As it happened, their gloom was unjustified. Early in 1831, the repeal bill was defeated in the House of Representatives. The vote against it was an overwhelming 183–51. The other anti-Court bills were also either voted down or abandoned.

There were several reasons for their defeat. One was that the Court's critics could not agree among themselves. Some condemned the Court for putting federal rights above states' rights but approved its probusiness decisions. Others had just the opposite reaction. Still others resented decisions that overturned laws in their own states but had no objection to the overturning of state laws elsewhere. Unable to agree on what the Court was doing wrong, they could not agree on how to change it.

But there was another reason the attacks on the Court failed. That reason had to do with the Court itself.

For the Supreme Court was changing. It was responding to Congress's anger, even though that anger did not take the form of a specific anti-Court law or amendment. Chief Justice Marshall, for instance, began making sure all seven justices were present to vote on constitutional questions. That took care of Senator Johnson's complaint about three-justice majorities.

Even more important, the Court was at last slipping from John Marshall's grip. The aging Federalist, seventy-six years old in 1831, had lost the ability to dominate the other justices.

Over his objections, they were beginning to hand down decisions that reflected Republican ideas. Some of these decisions weakened contract rights. Others went contrary to business interests. Increasingly, Marshall found himself in dissent.

The Chief Justice faced defiance off the bench as well. Much of it came from President Andrew Jackson. Jackson, elected in 1828, was the first president from a frontier state— Tennessee—and the first member of the new Democratic party to live in the White House. He opposed Marshall on most issues. Twice, he refused outright to obey Supreme Court rulings. "John Marshall has made his decision," Jackson is supposed to have said upon one occasion. "Now let him enforce it."

Whether or not the president used those words, his defiance was real. And as he knew, there was little the Court could do about it. Jackson's refusal to enforce Supreme Court decisions pointed up the Court's great weakness—its physical inability to compel the other branches of government to abide by its rulings. The Court has no police force to carry out its will. It commands no army. The Court's strength is a moral strength. It lies in the respect that we as a nation have for the Court and in the willingness of Americans to accept its decisions as law.

It was John Marshall who, almost single-handedly, won that respect for the Court. But now, the "Great Chief Justice" was passing from the scene. On June 6, 1835, he died.

To replace him, Jackson appointed Roger Brooke Taney, a fellow southerner and states' righter. Taney (he pronounced it TAW-ney) had no desire to tread in Marshall's activist footsteps. He intended instead to follow the path of "judicial restraint," deciding cases by looking at the facts in the narrowest possible sense. Unlike Marshall, Taney did not plan to break constitutional ground by claiming new powers for the Court or enlarging the rights of Congress or the president.

Taney's restraint and his devotion to state, rather than federal, rights helped improve the relationship between Congress and the Court. In 1837, Congress did pass a new Judiciary Act, but it was not a law aimed at limiting Supreme Court power. It created two new badly needed judicial circuits to hear cases around the West and Southwest. The act also added two seats to the Supreme Court, raising its membership to nine.

Congress-Court relations remained smooth over the next two decades. Then, on March 4, 1857, Taney announced a decision that was to tear the country apart.

Chief Justice

Roger B. Taney	1836-1864

Associate Justices

William Johnson	1804-1834
H. Brockholst Livingston	1807-1823
Thomas Todd	1807-1826
Gabriel Duvall	1811-1835
Joseph Story	1812-1845
Smith Thompson	1823-1843
Robert Trimble	1826-1828
John McLean	1830-1861
Henry Baldwin	1830-1844
James M. Wayne	1835-1867
Philip P. Barbour	1836-1841
John Catron	1837-1865
John McKinley	1838-1852
Peter V. Daniel	1842-1860
Samuel Nelson	1845-1872
Levi Woodbury	1845-1851
Robert C. Grier	1846-1870
Benjamin R. Curtis	1851-1857
John A. Campbell	1853-1861

4

The Difficult Years: Dred Scott and Reconstruction

Equal Justice Under Law. It's the Supreme Court's motto, but it was far from being a reality in nineteenth-century America.

American women were not equal. Like women in other countries, they were forbidden to vote or hold public office. In some places, American women did not even have the right to own or manage property or to have a say in the way their husbands chose to raise and educate their children.

Nor were the red-skinned native American "Indians" equal. They could be herded onto reservations and moved about from spot to spot to make room for white farmers and pioneers. Even white men who belonged to certain religious faiths could be legally discriminated against. In the nineteenth century, laws in several states kept non-Christians or non-Protestants from running for office or voting in elections.

But of all who stood unequal before the law, the lowliest and worst treated were America's black slaves. Slaves could be forced to labor in their white masters' fields, chop their wood and tend their livestock, prepare their food, clean their houses, and care for their children—all without receiving a cent in pay. At the same time, slaves could be bought, sold, whipped, or starved and the women raped and families torn apart—all quite legally.

The first slaves were brought to what is now the United States in 1619, and at first, slavery existed all over the country. By the 1800s, however, it was confined almost entirely to the southern states. Conditions there favored slavery. Plantations were large, and many hands were needed to harvest the crops of cotton and tobacco. The warm climate meant that plantation owners did not have to spend large amounts of money on their slaves' clothing and housing.

In the North it was different. Northern farms were smaller than southern plantations. The bulk of the North's wealth came from manufacturing, not from agriculture. However, setting slaves to work in the North's mills and factories would not have made good business sense. The area's harsh climate made warm clothes and snug dwellings a necessity most of the year. Any northern manufacturer who tried to operate on slave labor would have faced crushing expenses.

During the early years of the nineteenth century, tensions developed between North and South, between free states and slave states. Most southerners were defensive about what they called their "peculiar institution." They were convinced that freeing their slaves would spell economic ruin and the end of their gracious plantation life.

In the North, opposition to slavery was increasing. Some attacked the institution because they feared that slave-produced goods and crops could be sold more cheaply, and therefore more profitably, than their own goods and crops. Others had moral or religious grounds for wishing to abolish slavery. These so-called abolitionists carried on a vigorous campaign against it. One abolitionist goal was to free the slaves in the South. Another equally important one was to keep slavery out of the territories of the U.S. West and Southwest.

The abolitionists' effort to halt the spread of slavery met with fierce opposition. As each newly settled territory applied for statehood, southern representatives in Congress tried to get it admitted to the Union as a slave state. Northerners fought to keep it free. The result was one compromise after another.

The Missouri Compromise came first, in 1820. Congress passed legislation to create two new states: Missouri, slave, and Maine, free. The Missouri Compromise also barred slavery anywhere north of Missouri's southern border, as far west as the Rocky Mountains.

Other compromises followed. Arkansas became a slave state in 1836 and Michigan a free one in 1837. Eight years later, Florida and Texas came in on the slave side, then Wisconsin, Iowa, and California on the free. That made sixteen free states and only fifteen slave, which pleased the North and dismayed the South. However, Congress made it up to the South by promising that the whole Southwest would be opened up to the possibility of slavery. As states there joined the Union, their populations would decide for themselves whether to be slave or free. This, naturally, pleased the South and dismayed the North.

It was against this background of rivalry and tension that Chief Justice Roger Taney announced his decision in *Scott* v. *Sandford,* more commonly known as the Dred Scott case. The 1857 ruling has been called the worst ever handed down by the nation's highest court.

At first, the case seemed straightforward enough. Dred Scott, a slave, was the property of John Emerson, a U.S. Army doctor stationed in Missouri. In 1834, the doctor and his slave moved north to Illinois, then to the territories that were to become the states of Wisconsin and Minnesota. Under the Missouri Compromise and other laws, slavery was illegal in all three places. While in the North, Scott married and had children.

In 1838, Dr. Emerson took Scott back to Missouri. Thereafter, the doctor died, and Scott sued the widowed Mrs. Emerson for his freedom and that of his family. He claimed that their stay in free territory had made them free human beings. If Scott could win his case in court, Mrs. Emerson would owe him regular wages for his work ever since 1834.

Scott did win, and Mrs. Emerson appealed the decision to the state supreme court. There, she won.

Now complications entered the case. Mrs. Emerson remarried. Her new husband, C.C. Chafee, was a congressman from Massachusetts and a leading abolitionist. Fired by abolitionist sentiments herself, the former Mrs. Emerson agreed to an elaborate plan to try to get the federal courts to issue an antislavery ruling. She and Chafee arranged to sell Scott to her brother, J.F.A. Sanford of New York State. (Sanford is the "Sandford" in the case. His name was misspelled in official reports.) The sale of Scott was not a real sale, though, but a fake. Sanford, also an abolitionist, had no intention of holding Scott in servitude. Like the Chafees, he hoped to use the case to get the courts to declare that slaves became free as soon as they entered free territory.

On Monday, February 11, 1856, the nine justices of the U.S. Supreme Court began hearing arguments in *Scott* v. *Sandford*. The presentations lasted four days, and when they were over, the justices found that they had nine separate opinions about the case.

The simple solution would have been for them to dismiss Scott's case on a technical point: As a black, Scott could not be a citizen and therefore had no right to bring a legal suit in a court of law. The Supreme Court had ruled that way earlier in a similar case. But Taney was reluctant to stop there.

The Chief Justice was a southerner and a slave owner. He knew he had the votes to rule against Scott. Besides himself, four other southerners occupied seats on the high bench in 1856. Yet Taney also knew that two northern justices were planning to write outspoken dissents in the case. He feared those antislavery opinions might appear to have more moral weight than his own dismissal on a technicality. So instead of deciding the issue on very narrow grounds, Taney issued a broad ruling meant to establish the right of the slave states to promote their way of life throughout the territories.

That ruling declared the Missouri Compromise unconstitutional. According to the Fifth Amendment, no person may be deprived of property without "due process of law." Slaves were a form of property; "articles of merchandise" was how Taney expressed it. Like other kinds of property, slaves could not be taken from their owners without due process— formal legal proceedings. But the Missouri Compromise afforded slave owners no opportunity for such proceedings. It simply stated that people living in certain territories could not own slaves. Thus it illegally deprived slave owners like Dr. Emerson of that which belonged to them. It was this that made the compromise unconstitutional, Taney concluded.

In point of fact, the Missouri Compromise was no longer in effect when Taney issued his ruling. Congress had repealed it in 1854. But the ruling affected more than that one piece of legislation. It would apply to *any* attempt Congress might make to limit slavery. So the effect of the decision was to open all U.S. territories—northern, western, and southern—to the "peculiar institution."

The news fell like a bombshell on the North. It signaled the Court's determination to protect slavery while preventing Congress from doing anything to halt or control its spread. This horrified abolitionists, who realized that from now on they would not be able to fight slavery in the federal courts or legislature. It made abolitionists out of many who had previously been only lukewarm in their opposition to slavery. It brought thousands of people into the Republican party.

This Republican party was not Thomas Jefferson's old Republican party. It was a new group, founded in 1854 partly to oppose the spread of slavery. Among its members was a former congressman from Illinois named Abraham Lincoln. In May 1860, Republican leaders chose Lincoln to run for president, and the next November he was elected.

Lincoln's election horrified the South, much as the Dred Scott decision had horrified the North. One by one, the Southern states announced they were seceding—withdrawing—from the Union. Five weeks after Lincoln's March 1861 inauguration, southern troops fired on Union forces at Fort Sumter in Charleston, South Carolina. The Civil War had begun.

Not only did the Dred Scott decision play a role in starting the war, it also plunged the Supreme Court into disrepute. One New York newspaper cautioned, "If the people obey this decision they disobey God." Another maintained that the Court had "seriously impaired, if not destroyed" its "moral authority and consequent usefulness." In Congress, there was new talk of repealing Section 25 of the Judiciary Act of 1789, or of "punishing" the Court in some other way.

Six weeks after the Civil War began, Congress and the North were infuriated by another Taney ruling. This came in the case of Ex parte *Merryman*. *Ex parte* means "on one side only." It is an appeal to a court on behalf of just one party.

John Merryman, of Maryland, was accused of urging his state to secede and join the fighting on the side of the South. To federal officials, this was treason, and Merryman was arrested, thrown into a military prison, and held for trial before a military court.

Was this constitutional? Merryman and his friends claimed not. As a civilian, Merryman had a right to trial by jury in a civilian court, they said. An appeal was entered at the U.S. circuit court in Baltimore. The case came before Chief Justice Taney, who was presiding over that court as part of his circuit-riding responsibilities. Taney ruled that Merryman did have a constitutional right to trial in a civil courtroom. He ordered the prisoner released from the military jail.

Taney's order was ignored. The prison commander, acting on orders from Lincoln himself, refused to free Merryman. The Chief Justice could do nothing about it. *Merryman* was another reminder that the Supreme Court has no physical means of compelling the other branches of government to follow its rulings. Taney, already despised for his decision in the Dred Scott case, lacked the moral standing to win respect for his ruling in *Merryman*.

Even so, *Merryman* was a landmark decision. For the first time, the Court had ruled against the unconstitutional use of military police power. For the first time, it had upheld a citizen's individual liberty against the forces of government.

At the time, though, these points struck most people as trivial. In 1861, the country—that is, the twenty states that remained loyal to the Union—was on Lincoln's side, not Taney's. The nation was at war, the president's supporters said, fighting for its very existence. That made it the president's obligation to take any action he deemed necessary to win that war. Even if an executive order violated an individual's constitutional rights, that order could be justified by the demands of war.

So although people today may regard Taney's *Merryman* ruling as courageous, in 1861 it was just one more reason to criticize the Supreme Court. Congress was still discussing the idea of passing legislation to curb the Court. One senator even suggested "abolishing the present Supreme Court and establishing another Supreme Court."

But such radical action proved unnecessary, just as it had thirty years earlier when the Marshall Court had begun to change in response to congressional pressure. The Taney Court changed, too. In 1862, three associate justices left the bench, and their seats went to Republicans. The next year, Congress enlarged Court membership, and the president got to appoint yet another Republican. In 1864, Roger Taney died. Lincoln named Salmon P. Chase to replace him.

The year after Taney's death, the war ended. The Union had won; the country was whole again. Now Lincoln prepared to begin the delicate task of reconstructing the nation, of reconciling victorious North and war-torn South.

But that task was to fall to other hands. On April 14, 1865, just five days after the South surrendered, President Lincoln was shot and fatally wounded. He died the next day, and Vice-President Andrew Johnson took the oath of office. It was President Johnson who presided over Reconstruction.

Reconstruction began with the ratification of the Thirteenth Amendment to the Constitution. This amendment outlaws slavery. Two other amendments soon followed. The Fourteenth makes blacks citizens and forbids the states to deprive them, or any other persons, of "life, liberty, or property, without due process of law." The Fifteenth Amendment says the states could no longer keep citizens from voting because of their race or color.

The three Reconstruction amendments were positive amendments, aimed at giving real meaning to the words "Equal Justice Under Law." Other Reconstruction measures had a less idealistic purpose. Many northern congressmen desired to humiliate the South and make its states regret ever having seceded from the Union. These men cooperated in passing bills that placed the South under military rule and made it nearly impossible for southerners who had supported secession to regain control of their own state governments.

President Johnson and Congress quarreled bitterly over Reconstruction. When Johnson refused to sign various acts into law, Congress passed them over his veto. Congress also voted to reduce Supreme Court membership. It decided not to allow the next three Court vacancies to be filled. That meant that Johnson would have no opportunity to appoint justices who might be sympathetic to the South.

By 1868, the quarrel between president and Congress had reached a climax, and in February of that year, the House voted to impeach Johnson.

On March 5, the president went on trial in the Senate. Chief Justice Salmon P. Chase presided. The trial lasted over two months and ended in an acquittal—but only just. Johnson escaped conviction by a single vote.

The Supreme Court became enmeshed in other Reconstruction feuds. The sharpest clash between Congress and the Court erupted out of an 1866 case, Ex parte *Milligan.* This case, like *Merryman,* involved a civilian facing military trial. Again, the Court ruled that the Constitution decrees civilian trials for civilians.

As is usual with Supreme Court cases, *Milligan* had implications that went far beyond Lambdin Milligan himself. If it was unconstitutional for civilian Milligan to be subjected to military justice, then what about the hundreds of thousands of civilian southerners who were subject to the military rule Congress had established in their states? Would the Court decide that that rule was unconstitutional?

Just the thought that it might aroused Congress to fury. Once again, the old threats were trotted out: The justices would be impeached. Section 25 would be repealed. The judiciary would be reorganized. The Court's right to hear cases like *Milligan* and *Merryman* would be curtailed.

Congress actually carried out this last threat. In January 1868, the Court agreed to hear another case like Milligan's, this one known as Ex parte *McCardle.* In early March, the justices listened to the arguments. Eighteen days after that, Congress voted to remove cases like *McCardle* from Supreme Court jurisdiction.

The vote marked a low point for the Court. Of course, Congress had the right to do as it had done. Article 3 of the Constitution allows Congress to regulate Supreme Court jurisdiction.

But Article 3 does not give Congress the right to remove from the Court's jurisdiction a case that the justices have already heard. It does not say that the Court must abide by such an action. Yet the justices did abide by it. They lacked the courage to stand up to Congress and issue a ruling in *McCardle* during the eighteen days between the time they heard arguments and the time Congress voted to take the case away from them. Humbly, the Supreme Court bowed to Congress.

Soon it was to bow to a president. In March 1869, Johnson's term expired and Ulysses S. Grant was inaugurated. The next year, the Court accepted a case that involved a dispute about two different kinds of money—paper money and coins of gold.

The question in *Hepburn* v. *Griswold* was whether or not businessmen could use paper money—"greenbacks"—as "legal tender" to pay off their debts. Among those who favored paper money were the men who were building and running the nation's new railroad lines. Many of these men owed huge sums of money, and they preferred to pay in paper rather than in gold. Greenbacks were easier to come by than gold. They were worth less than gold, too. On the other side of the case were the creditors to whom the railroad men owed their debts. They were demanding to be repaid in the more valuable coins.

President Grant was firmly on the side of the railroaders, and he watched with great interest to see what the Court would do. In February 1870, he found out. The Court ruled against the railroads. Greenbacks could not be used as legal tender, the justices said.

That angered the president and a majority of congressmen. But a remedy was at hand, and they did not hesitate to seize it. Already, now that Andrew Johnson was no longer president, Congress had shifted Supreme Court membership back up to nine. On the very day the Court announced its decision in *Hepburn,* Grant sent the names of two new Court nominees to the Senate. Both were known to favor railroading interests, and both were speedily confirmed. Fifteen months later, the Court considered another greenback case. This time it ruled in favor of the cheap money, reversing the *Hepburn* decision.

Such a sudden reversal is extraordinarily rare. As a rule, Supreme Court justices do not overturn their own earlier decisions. They prefer to let those decisions remain as precedents to refer to and rely upon in making future rulings. Standing by their own precedents and being slow to change them are two ways the justices seek to build up respect for the Court and its findings.

But the Supreme Court of 1871 was not a Court suited to building respect for itself. Never had a Supreme Court ranked lower in public opinion. Never would one rank so low again. The damage that had begun in 1857 with the Dred Scott decision was complete. With the Legal Tender cases of 1870 and 1871, the Supreme Court appeared to be yielding its pride and abandoning its independence. It seemed to have become little more than a political tool of the other branches of government.

Chief Justices

Salmon P. Chase	1864-1873
Morrison R. Waite	1874-1888

Associate Justices

Nathan Clifford	1858-1881
Noah H. Swayne	1862-1881
Samuel F. Miller	1862-1890
David Davis	1862-1877
Stephen J. Field	1863-1897
William Strong	1870-1880
Joseph P. Bradley	1870-1892

5

The Court and Business

The years between 1857, the time of the Dred Scott decision, and 1871, when the Supreme Court caved in to political pressure and reversed itself in the Legal Tender cases, were bad ones for the Court. They were bad for the nation, too. The bitter split over slavery and other issues, a bloody civil war, and the harshness of Reconstruction all were crammed into those fourteen tragic years. But at last, as the country moved into the 1870s, the future looked brighter.

Although Reconstruction did not end officially until 1877, the worst of it was past by the early 1870s. Already, the eleven southern states that had seceded had been readmitted to the Union. In Congress, northern senators and representatives began to think less about punishing the South and more about really rebuilding it.

The Supreme Court was rebuilding as well. As the decade began, the justices were still enjoying the novelty of new, larger, more comfortable quarters. In 1860, they had moved out of the basement room in the U.S. Capitol that had become their home back in 1810. Now they were hearing cases in the stately hall that had been the Senate's until that body began meeting in another part of the building. The Supreme Court was to occupy the old Senate chamber until 1935.

In other ways, too, the Court's situation had improved. Its membership, which had hopscotched around from nine, to ten, to seven, and back to nine in just six years during the 1860s, finally stabilized. It has remained at nine since 1869.

The year 1869 also saw the end of circuit riding by Supreme Court justices. Circuit riding had been a tiresome chore, and the justices were pleased when Congress relieved them of it. They were pleased again two years later, when Congress raised their salaries to $8000 a year. The Chief Justice got $8500. Salmon P. Chase was the first Chief Justice to benefit from the increase. Two years later, in 1873, he died, and President Grant named Morrison R. Waite to succeed him.

Another change for the better lay ahead for the Court. This was a lightening of the justices' workload. By the 1880s, the Court was overwhelmed by cases waiting to be decided. Each new term began with between one thousand and two thousand cases listed on the docket. Many of the cases dealt with patents for new inventions. Finally, in 1891, Congress established a special patent court to handle them. It also created intermediate courts of appeal to take other routine cases off the Supreme Court's hands. The number of cases quickly dropped to under three hundred a year.

Things were also looking up for the Court in less material ways. As the nation moved away from the divisions and the anger of the Civil War years, public resentment toward the Court faded. A new era was beginning.

A new era—and a country vastly different from the one that had gained independence less than a century before. One difference had to do with population. In 1790, fewer than four million people lived in the United States. By 1870, there were thirty-eight million.

Natural population growth accounted for part of the increase, but another part was the result of immigration from other countries. Between 1821 and 1860, over five million men and women left their homelands to make new lives for themselves in the United States. During the 1860s alone, two and a half million more landed on American shores. The majority of the immigrants came from western Europe, particularly from the English-speaking nations of the British Isles.

An expanding population meant an expanding country.

By 1870, the thirteen original states had become thirty-seven. More people also meant more and bigger cities. In 1790, population density was sparse. A census taken that year showed only four and a half people per square mile of land. By 1870, there were almost eleven per square mile. Over 16 percent of all Americans lived in cities.

The economy was changing, too. In 1790, most Americans were farmers, craftsmen, or shopkeepers. By the mid-nineteenth century, manufacturing and industry were replacing farming as the nation's major source of wealth. Small businesses were turning into large companies or corporations. Mines, mills, and factories were opening up by the hundreds. At the outbreak of the Civil War, American businessmen had over a billion dollars invested in manufacturing. They were also putting huge sums of money—"capital"—into such modern means of transportation as railroads. There were fortunes to be made in railroading in the 1870s, and in America's other new business enterprises, too.

So that was the picture in 1870. A growing capitalist economy. Burgeoning cities and a rising population. A flood of immigration. The country had changed indeed. And it would continue to change in the years to come.

Population would go on rising. In 1900, it would be seventy-six million; thirty years later, 123 million.

Immigration would increase. Between 1871 and 1900, nearly twelve million new immigrants would enter this country. Over eighteen million more would arrive by 1930. The majority would not be English-speaking but would be from the nations of central, southern, and eastern Europe—from places like Germany, Italy, Poland, and Hungary. On the West coast, many would be from China and Japan.

The immigrants and the rising population were to fuel the new industrial economy. By 1900, manufacturing investment would be ten times what it had been in 1860—ten billion dollars. Americans would have become familiar with a new word—"millionaire." Millionaires were those capitalists clever enough and lucky enough to be wringing enormous profits out of the industrial expansion. Their lives were far different from the lives of the millions of men, women, and children who worked in their mines and factories and kept their plants and machines running smoothly and profitably. The capitalists' views of how the country should be managed and how its laws should operate were different from those of working people, too. It would be the Supreme Court that would stand between laborers and capitalists, interpreting the laws that governed both.

The central issue that separated working men and women from the capitalists who employed them was this: Should government be permitted to make laws to regulate business and to protect workers and consumers?

Capitalists thought not. Business must be free to operate without government regulation—government "interference," they called it. After all, it was business that was making the country rich and strong, providing Americans with more new jobs and more useful new products each year. And it was business that would make America even richer and stronger in the future—if only its leaders were allowed to run their own affairs in the way that seemed best to them. Such a let-business-alone-to-run-itself philosophy is known as laissez-faire. *Laissez-faire* is the French equivalent of "let them do as they choose." Most capitalists defend laissez-faire as the best way to ensure prosperity for everyone.

To others, laissez-faire is nothing more than a license that allows the rich and powerful to prey upon the poor and helpless. Under a system of strict laissez-faire, the former have nearly all the rights and privileges and the latter almost none. In the laissez-faire world of the 1870s, no law obliged employers to pay a decent wage. Employers were not required to protect their workers' health and safety. Laws permitted them to hire children as young as ten to work long hours at backbreaking jobs for a few cents a day.

Businessmen could charge exorbitantly high prices for necessary goods and services that only they could provide. People had to pay their prices or do without. Merchants were free to offer shoddy or worthless goods for sale. Unscrupulous men could process food under filthy conditions and market dangerous drugs as "medicines." If someone became ill or died after using one of their products, it was just too bad. The law did not forbid such practices.

Nor were there laws to protect workers' rights. Bosses could keep their workers from joining labor unions. Legally, they could fire employees who went on strike for higher pay or better working conditions. Or they could have the strikers thrown into jail. Under nineteenth-century laissez-faire capitalism, all the rules were tipped to favor wealth and business.

Some Americans wanted to change that. From time to time, lawmakers in Congress and in the state legislatures passed bills aimed at regulating certain aspects of business. As soon as each became law, it was challenged in court. One by one, the regulatory laws came up before the Supreme Court for review.

The Waite Court tended to let such laws stand. In 1877, the justices held that a state could limit the amount of money a businessman might charge customers who were dependent upon his services. The case, *Munn* v. *Illinois,* involved an Illinois law that set prices in Chicago slaughterhouses. The vote in favor of state regulation was 7–2.

In the long run, though, the minority opinion in *Munn* turned out to have a more lasting impact than the majority view. This is sometimes true in Supreme Court cases. A minority opinion may be largely ignored when it is written. But later, the Court may begin to change its mind about the issue involved. If that occurs, the old dissent may be remembered. It may even become the basis for new majority opinions.

This is what took place in *Munn.* Writing the Court's minority opinion, Associate Justice Stephen J. Field condemned the majority position. To tell a merchant how much he could charge was unconstitutional, the justice asserted. It was an attack upon his liberty and upon his right to use his property as he saw fit.

In 1877, Field's words were mere dicta—a justice's nonbinding opinion. Eleven years later, they were law.

During those eleven years, six new associate justices joined the Court. Five of them were appointed by Republican presidents. By the 1880s, the Republican party had come to be the party of wealth and business, and the new justices mirrored that orientation. In general, they were conservative men with a probusiness point of view. Several had been employed as lawyers for the nation's railroad companies. In 1888, the Court also got a new Chief Justice, Melville W. Fuller. He, too, was a former railroad attorney. With Fuller at its head and the new associates in their places, the Court renounced the position it had taken in favor of business regulation in *Munn*. Enthusiastically, the justices threw themselves behind laissez-faire capitalism.

For the rest of the nineteenth century and well into the twentieth, probusiness conservatives directed the Court. Their beliefs echoed those of Chief Justice John Marshall, that Federalist champion of wealth and property rights. Over the years, the Court overturned one business-regulation law after another. It refused to put an end to child labor, for instance. It struck down laws to limit working hours for adults. It freed employers from any responsibility to repay workers for injuries received on the job. It ruled that a state might not regulate railroad fares.

The railroad rate case was a milestone for the Court. Writing for the majority, Associate Justice Samuel Blatchford pointed out that the law in question allowed the state of Minnesota to decide what fares would be without giving the railroad company the right to appeal its decisions in court. This deprived the railroad of due process of law, Blatchford maintained. And that was a violation of the Fourteenth Amendment to the Constitution.

The Fourteenth Amendment? That was the amendment that granted the rights of citizenship to blacks and former slaves. What could it possibly have to do with the rights of a railroad company?

The Fuller Court answered the question imaginatively. According to the amendment, no "person" might be deprived of life, liberty, or property without due process. A corporation such as a railroad company was a "person," the justices said.

They were not being entirely illogical. The word *corporation* comes from the Latin *corpus,* "body." Yet even though this language link exists, the Supreme Court can be credited with ingenuity when it transformed an amendment intended to guarantee equality for blacks into a means of promoting laissez-faire capitalism!

The Court was less creative when it came to applying the Fourteenth Amendment to those it was actually intended to serve. As a rule, the Waite and Fuller Courts (and later Courts as well) showed themselves reluctant to protect the civil rights of black Americans.

A rare exception to that rule came in 1880. That year, the Court declared that blacks had the constitutional right to vote in federal elections. But when it came to state laws which restricted that right, the Court acted with great restraint. For example, state laws in the South required black voters to meet impossible educational standards. Whites in the same states did not have to meet the same standards. The Court refused to strike down such laws. Yet at the same time, the justices adopted a posture of judicial activism when it was a matter of federal laws aimed at guarding blacks' rights. Between 1876 and 1884, they managed to find constitutional grounds for upsetting three major civil rights laws.

Perhaps the single worst blow to black hopes and aspirations came in 1896 with the Court's decision in *Plessy* v. *Ferguson*. In this case, the Court examined a Louisiana law that called for railroads to provide separate seats and other accommodations for blacks and whites. The law was valid, the Court ruled. Accommodations might be separate, as long as they were equal.

The lone dissenter in *Plessy* was Associate Justice John Marshall Harlan. Harlan, like his namesake, served thirty-four years on the Court. His grandson, also named John Marshall Harlan, sat on the Court from 1955 to 1971.

Harlan had no doubt about what would happen if the decision in *Plessy* was allowed to stand. There would be "aggressions more or less brutal" against blacks around the country, he predicted. He was right. For the next sixty years, the doctrine of "separate but equal" made racial segregation—separation—the law of the land. It placed black men and women in an inferior category and made it easy for whites to keep them out of restaurants, hotels, swimming pools, and other public places. It also made it easy to keep blacks out of good schools and colleges, high-paying jobs, professional life, and much more. Such exclusion was the "less brutal" aggression. More brutal were beatings and lynchings—illegal hangings—that happened from time to time, especially in the South.

Court decisions unfavorable to blacks were accompanied by decisions unfavorable to other disadvantaged groups, such as the poor. In 1895, the Court was asked to rule on a federal income tax law. Under the law, no one earning less than $4000 a year would pay the tax. People earning more than $4000 would pay a tax amounting to 2 percent of their earnings.

The tax and its exemption were highly controversial. Congress had written the law and included the exemption to benefit the needy. But benefiting the needy meant hurting the well-to-do, said those who opposed the tax. Furthermore, they went on, the income tax required states with many wealthy people to pay more in taxes than states whose people were generally less well off. This was clearly unconstitutional. Article 10 of the Constitution declares that population, and population alone, is to determine how much tax each state pays. The more people in a state, the more the federal government can collect. But throughout the states, everyone must be taxed at the same rate. In the case of *Pollock* v. *Farmer's Loan & Trust Co.,* the Supreme Court accepted this argument, and America's poorest citizens continued to be taxed at the same rate as its richest ones. Not until 1913 did a federal income tax become legal. In that year, the states ratified the Sixteenth Amendment, which gave Congress the right to levy a tax based on wealth, rather than on population.

The justices also demonstrated their conservatism in the area of freedom of speech. Early in the twentieth century, a number of freedom-of-speech cases reached the Court. The cases grew out of laws passed in 1917 and 1918, when the United States was at war with Germany. These World War I laws made it a crime to criticize the United States, its government, its Constitution, its flag, or its armed forces. They also made it illegal to encourage young men to refuse to join the army. Several of those found guilty of breaking the laws appealed their convictions as far as the Supreme Court. The appeals were based upon the First Amendment, which guarantees freedom of speech.

The Supreme Court rejected the appeals and upheld the convictions. In the case of *Schenck* v. *U.S.,* for example, the Court ruled that the First Amendment did not protect an individual, Charles T. Schenck, who had urged men to resist being drafted into the army.

Yet even in confirming Schenck's conviction, the Court laid the groundwork for later decisions that would uphold Americans' First Amendment rights. Associate Justice Oliver Wendell Holmes, Jr., assigned to write the majority opinion, expressed the view that Schenck was guilty only because he had acted while the United States was at war. If he had urged draft resistance in peacetime, he would have been within his constitutional rights, Holmes declared. In an opinion that was to become a touchstone for later Courts, the justice wrote, "The question in every case is whether the words used . . . create a clear and present danger." In Schenck's case, the Court agreed that his words did present such a danger. But in other cases, Holmes warned, they might not.

Holmes's words "a clear and present danger" are remembered long after Schenck himself has been largely forgotten. Like Justice Field's dicta in *Munn* v. *Illinois,* they were to become the basis for very different decisions in the years to come. We will look at some of those decisions in Chapter 7.

Oliver Wendell Holmes, appointed to the Court by President Theodore Roosevelt in 1902, was one of its most outstanding justices. Holmes was unlike most of his fellow Court members, and looked upon the law differently than they did. To them, the law was rigid and unchanging, a set of rules that must be interpreted literally, no matter how they affected the human beings who lived under them. That is one reason the justices were able to rule against an end to child labor and other laissez-faire business practices. The Constitution said that no one might be deprived of liberty and property, and that was that.

Holmes had an alternate view of the law. To him, it was useful only insofar as it served society and helped people lead better, happier lives. The law must be flexible, Holmes thought. It must be adaptable, capable of changing with changing times and conditions. Twentieth-century America was not the America of 1787. The law must acknowledge that fact and reflect the changes that had taken place over a century and a quarter. This way of seeing things led Holmes into frequent dissent with Court decisions. "The Great Dissenter," many called him.

After 1916, Holmes was often joined in his dissent by Associate Justice Louis D. Brandeis. Brandeis, who sat on the Court until 1939, seven years after Holmes's retirement, shared Holmes's humane perspective. Occasionally, Holmes, Brandeis, or both together could persuade three other justices to go along with them. When that happened, business-regulation laws were upheld. The Court eventually accepted state laws that limited working hours for women, for instance. It also upheld the 1906 Pure Food and Drug Act, which set health standards for processing and manufacturing certain edible products.

When Holmes came onto the Court, Melville Fuller was still the Chief Justice. In 1910, Fuller died, and President William Howard Taft named Edward D. White to replace him. White served until 1921. When he died, President Warren G. Harding appointed former President Taft to succeed him. Taft was a very conservative Chief Justice. During his nine years on the Court, the justices overturned 141 state business-regulation laws. Taft died in 1930, and President Herbert Hoover chose Charles Evans Hughes as the new Chief Justice. Hughes had already spent six years as an associate justice.

The years between 1870 and 1930 had been relatively peaceful ones for the Court. Although social and economic reformers had criticized the justices for their conservative decisions, the criticism had not turned into an all-out attack upon the Court, as it had in the early 1800s and again during the Civil War and Reconstruction.

In fact, Congress actually broadened the Court's power during this period. Under a 1914 law, the Court won the right to accept cases in which a state supreme court had sustained a federal law. Before 1914, the Court heard only cases in which a federal law was overturned. The new law authorized the Supreme Court to issue a writ of certiorari—an order to a lower court to prepare a case for review—when it wished to examine such a state court decision. Eleven years later, Congress voted to give the Supreme Court more power to *refuse* to hear some cases the justices thought unimportant. Together, the new laws allowed the Court to pick and choose just those cases that seemed most significant.

Yet peaceful as the previous sixty years had been, the Court in 1930 stood at the brink of another historic confrontation with Congress and the president. Already, the seeds of that confrontation were sprouting.

Chief Justices

Melville W. Fuller	1888-1910
Edward D. White	1910-1921
William H. Taft	1921-1930
Charles E. Hughes	1930-1941

Associate Justices

Ward Hunt	1873-1882		
John M. Harlan	1877-1911	William H. Moody	1906-1910
William B. Woods	1881-1887	Horace H. Lurton	1910-1914
Stanley Matthews	1881-1889	Charles E. Hughes	1910-1916
Horace Gray	1882-1902	Willis Van Devanter	1911-1937
Samuel Blatchford	1882-1893	Joseph R. Lamar	1911-1916
Lucius Q. C. Lamar	1888-1893	Mahlon Pitney	1912-1922
David J. Brewer	1890-1910	James C. McReynolds	1914-1941
Henry B. Brown	1891-1906	Louis D. Brandeis	1916-1939
George Shiras, Jr.	1892-1903	John H. Clark	1916-1922
Howell E. Jackson	1893-1895	George Sutherland	1922-1938
Edward D. White	1894-1910	Pierce Butler	1923-1939
Rufus W. Peckham	1896-1909	Edward T. Sanford	1923-1930
Joseph McKenna	1898-1925	Harlan F. Stone	1925-1941
Oliver W. Holmes, Jr.	1902-1932	Owen J. Roberts	1930-1945
William R. Day	1903-1922	Benjamin N. Cardozo	1932-1938

6

The New Deal and Court Packing

On Wednesday, October 23, 1929, a panic hit Wall Street. Wall Street, in New York City, lies at the heart of one of the world's great financial centers. Many of the nation's largest corporations have their headquarters there. So do its leading stock exchanges. The exchanges are where stocks, or shares, in America's business enterprises are bought and sold.

On Wall Street, a panic means selling. Instead of wanting to buy shares in a business, everyone wants to get rid of them. Investors who are desperate to sell offer stocks at lower and lower prices. Their panic infects others, and soon those others are searching for buyers. But none can be found. Prices spiral downward.

What starts a panic? Often, no more than a rumor. Perhaps a story gets around that a business is in financial trouble. This upsets investors. Selling begins.

Most times, it ends quickly. People learn that the rumor is untrue. Or someone steps in and buys up the unwanted stock. This puts a halt to the selling and, if the rumor does prove false, earns the buyer a healthy profit. On October 23, though, the panic did not stop. On Thursday the twenty-fourth, it was worse, and it was worse still on the twenty-eighth. On the twenty-ninth—Black Tuesday—the market crashed.

One thing that made the crash of 1929 worse than other financial panics was that the economy had seemed so strong throughout the 1920s. Business had been booming, helped along, of course, by favorable Supreme Court decisions. Investors, who were already making huge amounts of money, wanted even more. So they bought more stock. Most paid for it with borrowed money.

By 1929, American investors were billions of dollars in debt. When the panic struck, lenders demanded payment. But those who had done the borrowing had no cash at hand. That meant that the lenders, who had borrowed from others in their turn, could not repay *their* debts.

It wasn't just individuals who were in debt—businesses, even large corporations, were, too. Many folded. Those that did not were still in deep trouble, and to save money, their owners began firing workers. Without jobs, the workers could not afford to feed and clothe their families. Hundreds of thousands of them lost their homes.

Hundreds of thousands also lost their life savings. Many banks, including the Bank of the United States, failed during the economic depression that followed the crash.

In the next months, the Great Depression tightened its grip on the nation. Stock market investors lost $50 billion in just two years. Between 1929 and 1932, national income dropped from $81 billion to $40 billion. Salaries and wages went from $49 billion to $29 billion. Farm income plummeted from $12 billion to $5 billion. Homeless men, women, and children roamed the countryside in search of work and food. Once-prosperous businessmen sold apples on city street corners. So did young college graduates.

In November 1932, in the depths of the Great Depression, the nation elected Franklin D. Roosevelt president. Roosevelt, a Democrat, was inaugurated the next March 4. He was the last president to be sworn in on that date. A few weeks earlier, the states had ratified the Twentieth Amendment, which pushed inauguration day back to January 20.

As a presidential candidate, Roosevelt had promised the country a "new deal." At once, he set about fulfilling that promise. During his first hundred days in the White House, he persuaded Congress to pass fifteen major New Deal laws. Other legislation followed, though at a slower rate.

Some New Deal laws were emergency measures, aimed at getting food to hungry Americans. Others sought to provide more lasting relief. New Deal laws created jobs and raised the prices farmers could get for their crops. They permitted more workers to join labor unions, and protected union members from antiunion bosses. They set up new rules for banks, businesses, and the stock market, rules that would make such deep depressions less likely in the future.

The New Deal was federal regulation on a grand scale, an attempt to tell business leaders all over the nation how to run their affairs. Like earlier regulatory laws, the New Deal laws were contested in the courts. By 1935, much of Roosevelt's economic program was up before the Supreme Court.

That same year saw new changes for the Court. During 1935, the Supreme Court left the Capitol for good and moved into a permanent home of its own. Besides a formal courtroom, the new Supreme Court building offered the justices such amenities as individual private office suites, robing and conference rooms, a law library, and a dining room. The justices' salaries measured up to the magnificence of their new surroundings. In 1935, associate justices earned $20,000 a year, a handsome sum by Depression standards.

It was in its spacious new home that the Supreme Court met to render a verdict on the New Deal. That verdict was unfavorable. In 1935 and the first half of 1936, the Court issued twelve anti–New Deal rulings. On one day alone, the Court declared two acts of Congress and one presidential order unconstitutional. Some of the anti–New Deal votes were unanimous. Others showed a split among the justices.

In finding against the New Deal, the justices made generous use of the Tenth Amendment. This amendment, the last in the Bill of Rights, reserves to the states all powers that the Constitution does not specifically assign to the federal government. Among the powers the Constitution does not give to Congress is the right to regulate business matters within the states. Therefore, the justices concluded, any such regulation is a matter each state must decide for itself.

But when a state did try to regulate its own business affairs, the justices called that unconstitutional as well. On June 6, 1936, for instance, the Court struck down a federal law that set basic minimum wages for working women. Five days later, it ruled against a New York state law that did exactly the same thing.

After the second decision was handed down, an associate justice who had voted with the minority in favor of wage regulation fired off an exasperated letter to his sister. "Our latest exploit was a holding . . . that there was no power in a state to regulate minimum wages for women," Justice Harlan F. Stone wrote indignantly. "The court last week said this could not be done by the national government, as the matter was local, and now it is said that it cannot be done by local governments even though it is local."

Justice Stone was not the only one feeling frustrated. Democrats in Congress were vexed at seeing their work systematically destroyed by the Court. "How much longer will we let the Supreme Court . . . pervert democratic processes?" one demanded. Another thought that Congress might soon "dethrone" the Court. Even Republicans, who usually favored the rights of business over those of labor, questioned some court decisions. Before the 1936 presidential election, Republican leaders announced their belief that laws abolishing child labor and protecting working women were perfectly constitutional.

Congress's anger over the justices' anti–New Deal stance led, once again, to a discussion of ways the power of the Court might be curbed. By 1937, 150 anti-Court proposals had been introduced in Congress. They included old, familiar ideas that had been around since the days of Chief Justice Marshall: limiting the Court's right to judicial review, requiring a majority of seven to declare an act of Congress unconstitutional, and turning federal judgeships into elective offices.

None of the bills became law, however. President Roosevelt saved the day for the Court.

He didn't mean to. Angry as Congress was at the Supreme Court, the president was even angrier. The justices were old-fashioned and hidebound, he fumed. Six of the nine were seventy years old or more, and it seemed unlikely that they would ever change their minds about the New Deal. Bitterly, Roosevelt denounced the "nine old men" who were obstructing his efforts to lead the nation out of the Depression. On February 5, 1937, he sent a Court-curbing proposal of his own to Congress.

It was a scheme to pack the Court. Under the president's plan, he would name a new justice to the bench for every sitting justice with ten years of service who had reached age seventy without retiring. Since six members of the Court already met this description, Roosevelt's plan would give him the immediate opportunity to increase the Court's size to fifteen. It would let him fill the six new seats with men he knew would back the New Deal. Added to the two or three justices who already occasionally voted for New Deal programs, this would give the president a majority on the Court.

Roosevelt's Court-packing plan was greeted with dismay. Practically every newspaper in the country condemned it. Public opinion polls revealed that ordinary citizens opposed the plan by a margin of nine to one.

The proposal also got off to a bad start in Congress. When it was read aloud in the Senate, Roosevelt's own vice-president, John Nance Garner, indicated his reaction by holding his nose and giving the "thumbs-down" sign. Conservative Republicans attacked the plan. So, to the president's surprise, did a number of liberal Democrats.

One reason for the opposition was that people objected to tampering with a Court that they respected, even when they disagreed with some of its decisions. Another was that Roosevelt had not acted forthrightly in the matter. Rather than admit that he wanted to pack the Court in order to turn it around politically, he pretended to be concerned that the nine justices had too much work to do. More were needed to handle all the cases they ought to be hearing, he insisted.

Few believed he was being sincere. Chief Justice Hughes drew up a report showing that the Court was hearing all the important cases that came its way. Enlarging it would be inefficient, he said, because it would mean "more judges to hear, more judges to confer, more judges to be convinced and to decide." Congress agreed. In July, it let the Court-packing bill die. The other 150 anti-Court proposals in Congress died, too. Roosevelt's offensive against the Court had made Court defenders out of some of its severest critics.

Nevertheless, Roosevelt got his way. Once again, as in the nineteenth century, the Court responded to pressure from the other branches of government. One conservative justice changed his position on a key New Deal issue. Another resigned in 1937, and three more left the bench in the two years after that. In all, Franklin Roosevelt got to appoint eight associate justices and one Chief Justice—more than any other president except George Washington. Among the most noteworthy of his appointments were Associate Justices Hugo L. Black, Felix Frankfurter, and William O. Douglas. The man Roosevelt named as Chief Justice was Harlan F. Stone. Stone, an associate justice since 1925, served as head of the Court from 1941 to 1945.

The Court had reversed itself on the New Deal long before all nine Roosevelt appointees were on the bench, however. Wags called its sudden turnabout "the switch in time that saved nine." Now the justices were finding *for* state and federal business regulation, *for* the rights of workers, and *against* unbridled laissez-faire capitalism. After 1941, the Court seemed to all but forget the Tenth Amendment. Instead, it referred to the precedent of John Marshall's opinion in *Gibbons* v. *Ogden*.

In that 1824 decision, Marshall had called attention to the phrase in the Constitution which authorized Congress to "regulate commerce . . . among the several States." In twentieth-century America, the Court held, almost all business transactions take place among the states. A product manufactured in one will probably be sold in the rest. It may be produced using raw materials, machinery, and equipment from other parts of the country. The fact that an article's production and distribution involves interstate commerce allows the federal government to oversee and regulate every aspect of its manufacture and sale, the Court ruled. Even farming, long considered a purely local activity, was now seen as entailing interstate commerce.

By the end of the 1930s, the Court was showing a more liberal attitude in nonbusiness cases as well. Such cases fell into three categories: First Amendment freedoms and the rights of citizenship, due process of law for persons accused of crimes, and civil rights for blacks.

As a matter of fact, the first hints of the trend toward liberalism in such areas had begun even before President Roosevelt launched his onslaught against the Court. Already, the justices were starting to extend the scope of certain of the freedoms guaranteed by the First Amendment.

The 1931 case of *Near* v. *Minnesota,* for instance, revolved around a Minnesota law designed to keep a newspaper there from publishing a series of articles about official crime and corruption in the state. The Supreme Court ruled against the state law. It was unconstitutional, the justices said, because it violated that part of the First Amendment that guarantees freedom of speech and of the press.

Never before had the Court declared so firmly that the First Amendment applies to state governments as well as to the federal government. That is because the amendment says only that *Congress* shall make no law that limits people's right to freedom of speech, of the press, and of religion. It does not mention the states.

But other amendments do. According to the Fourteenth Amendment, no state may pass a law that denies a person due process of law. What is that but an order to the states to respect people's First Amendment rights? Minnesota's censorship law was a clear defiance of that order, the justices ruled.

Time passed, and the movement toward a broader interpretation of the First Amendment continued. Even after the

United States entered World War II in 1941, the justices stood up for Americans' right to criticize their government and its conduct of the war. This was in contrast to the Court's position in such World War I cases as *Schenck* v. *U.S.* It demonstrated the justices' new willingness to distinguish between the free expression of an opinion and words that presented what Oliver Wendell Holmes had called "a clear and present danger." Associate Justices Hugo Black and William O. Douglas were the strongest advocates of extending the First Amendment right of freedom of speech.

The Court also began showing more sensitivity toward another First Amendment right—the right to freedom of religion. In 1943, the justices ruled that public school officials could not force the children of Jehovah's Witnesses to recite the Pledge of Allegiance. It is against the Witnesses' religious beliefs to salute a flag, and those beliefs must be respected, the Court held. This was a change for the Court. Three years before, in 1940, the justices had ruled against Jehovah's Witnesses in an almost identical case.

Yet the justices' position on people's rights was far from being absolute. During World War II, when the United States was at war with Germany and Japan, U.S. Army officials rounded up thousands of Japanese-Americans and confined them in special camps. The reasoning behind such activity was that Americans of Japanese ancestry posed a threat to the nation's security. Twice, in *Hirabayashi* v. *U.S.* and in *Korematsu* v. *U.S.,* the Supreme Court backed the policies against the Japanese-Americans. Today it is agreed that the roundups and detentions were unnecessary—Japanese-Americans were as loyal as any other Americans during the war—and absolutely unconstitutional.

The war ended in 1945. But even with the fighting over, many Americans felt they were still engaged in a war. This "war" was an angry rivalry between the United States and the Soviet Union.

Unlike the United States, the Soviet Union has a communist economy. That means that the country's means of production—its mines, factories, mills, and the like—are owned and run by the government. So are its shops and stores, its railroads and airlines—everything is under state control. The people of the Soviet Union live under rigid state control, too. The Soviet government is a dictatorship. It permits no free elections, and the vast majority of Soviet citizens are forbidden to take part in government or even to criticize it. To many Americans, with their traditions of democracy, capitalism, and free enterprise, communism seemed a terrible threat, a way of life that might one day engulf the United States.

Some Americans, in fact, became so afraid Soviet communists might seek to impose their system in this country that Congress and the states passed a number of harsh anticommunist laws. These laws made it a crime to promote communist ideas. Some kept people who had once been members of the Communist party from getting jobs—or from keeping the jobs they had. In later years, most Americans came to feel that the communist threat had been greatly exaggerated in the 1940s and 1950s. It never had presented a "clear and present danger" to the country. The anticommunist laws had been a terrible invasion of people's First Amendment rights. But at the time, the Supreme Court upheld those laws.

A second major category of nonbusiness cases considered by the court concerned the rights of people accused of crimes. One case, *Powell* v. *Alabama,* arose in 1932. Here, the Court ruled that the state of Alabama had acted unconstitutionally when it allowed a man who had no money, could neither read nor write, and was mentally deficient to be condemned to death without having a lawyer to speak for him in court. The case helped establish the right of a person on trial for his or her life to be represented by an attorney.

In another defendants' rights case, *Brown* v. *Mississippi,* the Court overturned the convictions of three men who had confessed to a crime after police had whipped and beaten them. *Brown* and *Powell* set basic standards for citizens' fair treatment by police and the courts. They were to become precedents for later decisions that would further enlarge the rights of defendants.

A third major group of cases involved the rights of American blacks. In 1932, *Norris* v. *Alabama* secured them the right to be picked as members of a jury. Overall, though, equal rights were a long way away for most black men and women. In 1935, in *Grovey* v. *Townsend,* the Supreme Court found that Democratic party officials in Texas had acted legally when they kept blacks from becoming party members. If it had been a state law that had kept them out of the Democratic party, the justices said, that would have been unconstitutional under the Fourteenth Amendment. But discrimination by private individuals was allowable. As a result, thousands of blacks continued to be cut off from the nation's political life. In Texas, and in other states of the Deep South, the Democratic party was all-powerful in 1935. A person had to be a party member in order to take part in politics.

Only slowly did the Court's position change. In *Shelley* v. *Kraemer,* the Court considered an agreement by white homeowners not to sell their houses to black families. Such agreements used to be common. They were made in the belief that if even one black moved into a "white neighborhood," all the whites would want to leave. Anxious to sell their homes, they would offer them at ridiculously low prices. That would mean everyone else's house would end up being worth less, too.

In *Shelley* v. *Kraemer,* the Court ruled against such agreements. True, a no-sale-to-blacks agreement is a private arrangement. But selling a house involves a formal written contract, a contract that the state will enforce if necessary, (if the buyer cannot pay, for example, or if the seller turns out to have lied about the condition of the house). That makes the sale of a house and the conditions of its sale a state matter. Under the Fourteenth Amendment, a state may not be bound by conditions that infringe upon the rights of individuals.

By the time the Supreme Court ruled in *Shelley,* it had a new Chief Justice, Frederick M. Vinson. Vinson was named to the Court in 1946 by President Harry S Truman. Under his leadership, the Court widened its use of the Fourteenth Amendment to enable blacks to enjoy the rights that should have been theirs under the Constitution. Several times, the

Vinson Court ordered blacks to be admitted to segregated public colleges and universities, for example. In one case, the justices told the state of Oklahoma to accept a qualified black at the state's all-white public law school—or build a whole new law school just for him! Blacks, encouraged by such decisions, brought more and more suits against discrimination by whites.

Then, in 1953, came *Brown* v. *Board of Education of Topeka.* The Court's decision in this case was to upset segregation laws around the country. It was to remake American society.

Chief Justices

Harlan F. Stone	1941-1946
Frederick M. Vinson	1946-1953

Associate Justices

Hugo L. Black	1937-1971
Stanley F. Reed	1938-1957
Felix Frankfurter	1939-1962
William O. Douglas	1939-1975
Frank Murphy	1940-1949
James F. Byrnes	1941-1942
Robert H. Jackson	1941-1954
Wiley B. Rutledge	1943-1949
Harold H. Burton	1945-1958
Tom C. Clark	1949-1967
Sherman Minton	1949-1956

7

The Warren and Burger Courts

Brown v. *Board of Education* was a direct attack upon the principle of "separate but equal." Separate but equal had been the rule for black Americans ever since the Supreme Court's 1896 decision in *Plessy* v. *Ferguson.* But as every black man and woman knew, separate but equal did not mean what it said. It meant separate—and *un*equal.

Even as children, blacks felt the inequality. Ten-year-old Linda Brown of Topeka, Kansas, felt it. For Linda, being black meant that she could not attend the public school near her home. Instead, Topeka school officials said, Linda must travel to an all-black school in another part of town.

Most black schools were depressing places. They were older and less attractive than white schools. The buildings were dilapidated, the classrooms dingy, the equipment missing or damaged. Schoolbooks were likely to be hand-me-downs, passed on from white schools when students there got bright new texts.

Knowing that the situation was unfair, and worried about the quality of the education his daughter was getting, Linda's father brought suit against the Topeka board of education. He asked the courts to order the board to admit Linda to the local white school.

By 1953, *Brown* v. *Board of Education* had reached the Supreme Court. As we saw in Chapter 6, the Vinson Court had found in favor of blacks in several antidiscrimination cases. Even so, the Court did not seem ready to take the final step and overturn the precedent set in *Plessy*. In mid-1953, observers agreed, the justices stood 5–4 against ordering a sweeping end to segregation laws.

Then, in September, Chief Justice Vinson suddenly died. The next month, President Dwight D. Eisenhower named Earl Warren to succeed him. Warren, a former governor of California, was confirmed by the Senate early in 1954.

Warren took his seat—and transformed the Court. Within weeks, the justices had met to decide *Brown* v. *Board of Education*. On May 17, 1954, they announced that decision. Unanimously, they outlawed school segregation in Topeka and in every other public school district in the United States. How had Warren done it?

The answer was that Earl Warren was a compelling leader, the most forceful and persuasive Chief Justice since John Marshall. Like Marshall, Warren felt he had a mission to perform. For Marshall, that mission had been to establish the Constitution as the supreme law of the land, to promote the federal system, and to get the three branches of government working smoothly together. For Warren, the mission was making the old American dream of liberty, justice, and equality an everyday reality for all citizens, regardless of race, religion, color, ethnic (national) background, income, social position, health, education, or any other factor.

To carry out his mission, Warren was not content to rely upon the law only as it is written down in thick and dusty volumes. Marshall hadn't been, either. Both were judicial activists. Each searched for ways to use the law creatively to impose his vision of society upon the nation.

Of course Warren and Marshall lived in very different times, and their visions of society and of the nations were very different, too. So were the tools they each had to work with. As a man of the twentieth century, Warren had tools that Marshall had never heard of. They included psychology, the study of human thought and behavior, and sociology, the study of how human beings live together in society. Never did

Warren employ the lessons of psychology and sociology more effectively than when he turned the Court around in *Brown* v. *Board of Education.*

Separate but equal was a myth, Warren told his fellow justices. What was more, it could never be more than a myth, no matter how generously the law was administered. Let Topeka school officials pour millions of dollars into the city's black schools. Let them repair the buildings, fix up the classrooms, and buy the latest books and equipment. Linda and her classmates would still be apart, separated from the white majority.

This apartness would signal to them the belief of many whites that blacks are members of an inferior race. The sense of inferiority would enter the black children's minds and hearts, slowing their learning and making it impossible for them to go into the world feeling confident and able to succeed. Psychological studies had shown this to be true, Warren informed the justices, and his conviction persuaded them. "Separate educational facilities are inherently unequal," the justices wrote.

The decision in *Brown* was followed by other desegregation orders. Within two years, the Court had forbidden racial discrimination on the nation's public beaches and in its bathhouses, on public golf courses, and on city buses.

Besides taking an active stand on civil rights, the Warren Court interested itself in securing the constitutional rights of other disadvantaged Americans. In 1955, the justices took up the issue of the rights of poor people accused of, or convicted of, committing a crime. *Griffin* v. *Illinois* involved a man who was unable to appeal his conviction because he could not afford to pay for a typed transcript of his trial. The question before the Court: May a person too poor to pay for a transcript be forced to sacrifice his constitutional right to have his appeal heard?

The justices' answer was "No." If an appellant—a person who appeals—cannot afford a transcript, the state must bear the cost. "In criminal trials, a State can no more discriminate on account of poverty than on account of religion, race, or color," Justice Hugo Black wrote for the majority. "Plainly the ability to pay costs . . . bears no rational relationship to a defendant's guilt or innocence.''

The Warren Court also waded enthusiastically into the area of First Amendment rights. It was more liberal than any earlier Court had been in protecting Americans' freedom of speech. In the 1957 case of *Yates* v. *U.S.*, the justices went so far as to rule that even a person who advocates the overthrow of the federal government is within his First Amendment rights. Only if the speaker's words are tied to a specific violent action, such as assassinating a president or seizing the U.S. Capitol, do they present "a clear and present danger." However, the justices stopped short of declaring that the First Amendment protects all speech all the time. In *Roth* v. *U.S.*, also decided in 1957, they decided that it does not shelter the publication of pornographic or obscene material.

Even communists are entitled to First Amendment rights, the Court said. That was a departure from the Vinson Court practice of upholding the country's stringent anticommunist laws. It was also an unpopular position to take in the 1950s, but Chief Justice Warren did not let that bother him. By its ruling in one single case, *Pennsylvania* v. *Nelson,* the Court overturned anticommunist laws in forty-two states. The justices also said that people could not be fired from their jobs just because they were, or had been, communists. Unless an individual was in a "sensitive" position—if his or her work involved knowing military secrets, for example—party membership could not be grounds for dismissal.

By 1957, the Court's liberalism was leading it into new controversies. *Jencks* v. *U.S.* set the Court on a collision course with the Federal Bureau of Investigation. In *Jencks,* the justices ruled that if a man is convicted of a crime because of evidence brought by a government agency such as the F.B.I., he has the right to obtain records of that evidence to use in appealing his conviction. Not only did the *Jencks* ruling irritate F.B.I. officials, it aroused the ire of the bureau's many congressional supporters.

Another 1957 case brought the Court up against Congress itself. With their decision in *Watkins* v. *U.S.,* the justices took on the powerful Un-American Activities Committee of the

House of Representatives. This committee was devoted to investigating Americans suspected of taking part in or knowing about communist activity anywhere in the country. Hundreds of men and women (most of them quite harmless, as later became apparent) were brought before the committee and questioned in detail about their past lives, their private beliefs, and their friends and acquaintances. Any who refused to answer might be jailed.

Writing the majority opinion in *Watkins,* Warren vigorously assailed the committee's tactics. They amounted to "a new kind of congressional inquiry . . . a broadscale intrusion into the lives and affairs of private citizens," he said. The Chief Justice ordered an end to the committee's unconstitutional tactics.

That raised hackles in Congress. Leading anticommunists were outraged. "How much longer will this Congress continue to permit the Supreme Court to . . . protect the Communist party?" demanded Representative George Andrews of Alabama. States' righters were incensed as well. "It is only a question of time before the states will be deprived of all power and sovereignty," cried Representative Noah Mason of Illinois.

Then there were those who thought that the Court was taking too much authority upon itself. Representative James Davis of Georgia spoke of the Court's effort to achieve "a complete judicial dictatorship." In the Senate, Karl Mundt of North Dakota suggested that the Supreme Court was "endeavoring to become a legislative body." Strom Thurmond of South Carolina threatened the Court directly. "Congress must take action to limit the power of the Court," he declared. Part of Thurmond's anger was over decisions like those in *Jencks* and *Watkins.* But more of it may have been due to the Court's antisegregation rulings. Diehard segregationists—Thurmond was one—were determined to thwart the Court's obvious goal of desegregating American life.

Chief Justice Warren was a special target for the Court's enemies. Many spoke of impeaching him. President Eisenhower expressed regret at having appointed him to the bench.

"Biggest damnfool mistake I ever made," the president grumbled. Another justice frequently mentioned in connection with impeachment was William O. Douglas.

As usual during battles between the Court and Congress, dozens of Court-curbing bills were introduced in the House and Senate. They ran the gamut from bills of impeachment, to plans under which Congress would have the power to reverse some Court decisions, to limits on Supreme Court jurisdiction, to changes in the way justices were picked and approved. Only one passed, a bill originally aimed at overturning the Court's ruling in *Jencks*. Between the time the bill was introduced and the time it became law, however, it was watered down. In the end, it did little more than ratify the Court's decision in the case.

A much harsher anti-Court proposal was the Jenner bill. Introduced in July 1957 by Senator William E. Jenner of Indiana, the bill would have ended Supreme Court jurisdiction over cases involving possible communist subversion. In the process, it would have undone most of the Warren Court's civil liberties decisions. Although the bill made it through the House, it died in the Senate. Many thought its failure was due to the senators' feeling that the bill went too far. If passed, the Jenner bill would have weakened the Court seriously. A powerless Court might not be able to maintain its place as one of three equal branches of government, the senators believed. It might even lose the right of judicial review. This risk was one that few of even the angriest senators were willing to take.

Again, as in the past, a direct attack on the Court had fizzled. But as we have seen, even an unsuccessful attack is usually followed by a shift on the part of the justices. Confidently, the states' righters, segregationists, and militant anti-communists of the late 1950s waited for the pattern to repeat itself. The Warren Court was sure to begin reversing its decisions, they thought.

They were wrong. Although the Court did reject several civil liberties claims in 1957 and 1958, it quickly recovered its nerve and kept on down the road Earl Warren had laid out for it. Treading this path became easier when Americans elected liberal Democrat John F. Kennedy as president in 1960. More liberals were elected to Congress that year too.

In the 1960s, civil rights cases continued to come before the Court. Midway through the decade, the justices upheld Congress's Civil Rights Act of 1964. This law prohibited racial, ethnic, or religious discrimination in any place covered by the rules of interstate commerce. That included just about every place of business across the length and breadth of the United States—restaurants, hotels, movie theaters, the lot. John Marshall, a slave owner, would have been amazed to see how his 1824 ruling in *Gibbons* v. *Ogden* was being applied to black Americans 140 years later! The 1964 Civil Rights Act also said that employers could no longer turn people down for jobs because of their color, race, religion, or place of national origin. Anyone who broke the law would be subject to a suit brought by the U.S. government.

In another 1964 case, the Court examined a more subtle form of discrimination: a legal but unscrupulous way of limiting black representation in Congress and in the state legislatures. Whites managed the unequal representation by drawing election districts in ways that divided large black neighborhoods or communities into small sections. Once a black community was broken up, each small piece of it was added to a larger white area. This meant that blacks ended up being in the minority in nearly every district. Black candidates were rarely if ever elected. In *Reynolds* v. *Sims,* the court ruled that this practice must end. Black voters must have the same opportunity to elect their candidates that white voters did, the justices said.

Three years after the *Reynolds* decision, the impact of some of the justices' civil rights rulings affected the court directly. In 1967, the Supreme Court got its first black justice, Thurgood Marshall.

Civil rights was not the only area in which the Warren Court continued to make history. In the 1962 case of *Engel* v. *Vitale,* the justices ruled that public school students may not be asked to recite a prayer at the beginning of each school day. Most school prayers, such as the Lord's Prayer, were

Christian, the Court noted. Yet many American school-children belong to non-Christian faiths or to no faith at all. Forcing them to recite or listen to Christian devotions is a violation of their freedom of religion. It is also an unconstitutional mixing of government and religion, the justices said. The First Amendment forbids government to do anything to promote or "establish" any particular religion.

The Warren Court also pursued its interest in defendants' rights. In 1963, it ruled that if an accused person cannot afford to hire a lawyer, the state must provide one free of charge. In a pair of cases, *Escobedo* v. *Illinois* and *Miranda* v. *Arizona,* the justices further extended the rights of the accused. *Escobedo,* decided in 1964, established a person's right to see a lawyer before answering police questions about a crime. Two years later, in *Miranda,* the justices spelled out exactly what police officers around the country must do to protect the constitutional rights of those they arrest on suspicion of having committed a crime. To begin with, the police must tell a suspect, in clear and simple language, that he or she has the right to remain silent and not to answer questions. They must also inform the accused that anything he or she does say may later be repeated in a court of law. Finally, a suspect must be advised of his or her right to be represented by an attorney from the very start of the case.

Another matter that occupied Chief Justice Warren was the 1963 assassination of President Kennedy. On November 22 of that year, the president was shot and killed in Dallas, Texas. A young man named Lee Harvey Oswald had fired the gun. But had Oswald acted on his own? Or was he the front man for a conspiracy—a conspiracy that perhaps included high government officials?

Rumors of such a conspiracy were heard on all sides, and the new president, Lyndon B. Johnson, asked Warren to head a commission to investigate them. After a thorough probe, the Warren Commission reported its findings that Oswald had been the only one involved in Kennedy's death.

As the 1960s drew to a close, the Warren Court could look back upon nearly a decade and a half of extraordinary achievement. Thanks to the Chief Justice's activism and to his forward-looking vision of American society, the country had changed tremendously. Segregation seemed to be giving way to integration. The law had become more equal for rich and poor, powerful and weak. Americans had never enjoyed such broad First Amendment rights.

By now, though, the end was approaching for the Warren Court. Anti-Court sentiment was building up again. During the 1968 presidential election campaign, Republican party candidate Richard M. Nixon lashed out at the justices. Nixon promised that if voters elected him, one of his first priorities would be changing the Court's liberalism. When vacancies occurred, he would fill them with men who believed in judicial restraint. His justices would abide strictly by the letter of the Constitution. They would not try to stretch its meaning, to twist its words in order to justify one startling legal innovation after another.

Nixon got the chance he wanted to remake the Court. He was elected in 1968 and sworn into office in January 1969. In June, Earl Warren, then almost eighty years old, resigned. Nixon appointed a Minnesota lawyer and U.S. District Court of Appeals judge, Warren Burger, as Chief Justice. Burger's conservative views were similar to Nixon's own.

President Nixon had the opportunity to make a second Court appointment that same year. His first two choices for the seat were rejected by the Senate. Finally, in May 1970, the vacancy was filled by Harry A. Blackmun. Two years later, Nixon named a third justice, William H. Rehnquist.

Under Burger's leadership, the Supreme Court lost the sense of direction it had had when Earl Warren was Chief Justice. Nixon had hoped to make the Court more conservative. To some extent, he succeeded. The Burger Court drew back from Warren Court positions in several areas, particularly in cases having to do with the rights of the accused.

Yet the Burger Court was not consistently conservative. Some called it "quirky" or "unpredictable." Many of its decisions reinforced the Warren Court's extension of civil liberties and the rights of individuals. In 1972, for instance, the Court struck down state laws that permitted the execution of criminals. The laws were being enforced unfairly and unevenly, the justices found. A crime that meant death for one person might mean only jail for another. This was a violation of the Eighth Amendment, which forbids "cruel and unusual punishments." By the end of the 1970s, though, many states had rewritten their death penalty laws so that they reflected the Supreme Court's idea of fairness and evenness. The Burger Court showed its conservative side when it allowed these new laws to stand.

Still, remnants of Warren Court liberalism survived. In 1971, the Burger Court confirmed First Amendment rights when it ruled in *New York Times Co.* v. *U.S.* The case involved a *New York Times* reporter who obtained a set of secret U.S. military files. The government asked the Court to order the *Times* not to print the information in the files. The Court refused. The government's right to keep the information private was outweighed by the people's right to know about it, the justices decreed.

Two years later, in the highly emotional case of *Roe* v. *Wade,* the justices ruled that a state cannot prevent pregnant women from having abortions. Abortion is a private matter to be decided between a patient and her doctor, they said, and government may not intrude upon that decision. Only in the last three months of pregnancy, when an unborn child has a good chance of living outside the womb, may abortion be outlawed. It was Nixon appointee Harry Blackmun who wrote the majority opinion in *Roe* v. *Wade.*

In civil rights cases, too, the Burger Court took a line that was more liberal than some expected—or hoped for. One problem local officials ran into when they tried to obey Supreme Court school desegregation orders was that segregation of entire neighborhoods made it difficult to integrate local schools. Most black children lived in one part of town. Most white children lived in another. To educate black and white together often meant transporting children long distances by bus to and from their homes. Busing was a controversial topic in the 1970s. Even many who approved of its aim worried about young children undergoing one- or two-hour-long bus rides morning and evening. Despite the doubts, the Burger Court okayed busing.

The court approved other rather awkward arrangements designed to bring about equality for blacks and members of other minority groups. In *Regents of the University of California* v. *Allan Bakke,* the Court decided that it is all right for a college to give special consideration to minority-group applicants. That is, it may accept such applicants even when their marks are lower than the marks of whites who are rejected. Many whites, Allan Bakke among them, argued that such favoritism is unjust. But the Court held that it is a legitimate way of trying to make up for past racial discrimination.

Bakke was decided in 1978. The next year, the Court extended a similar policy of racial favoritism to business and industry. Employers may be encouraged to give preference to black job hunters, the justices ruled. Women are also covered by the decision in this case, *United Steelworkers of America* v. *Weber.* Women, like blacks, have long been treated as inferiors, the Court agreed. It is only right for businessmen to try to make up for some of that treatment through "affirmative action."

By the time the Court decided the two affirmative action cases, Richard Nixon was no longer president. He had resigned from office on August 9, 1974, climaxing one of the most spectacular conflicts ever to have taken place among the branches of government.

The conflict began during the 1972 presidential campaign. President Nixon was a candidate for reelection. In June, seven men employed by his reelection committee were arrested after they broke into the Washington, D.C., headquarters of the Democratic party. The Democratic offices were in the Watergate Hotel overlooking the Potomac River.

Throughout 1972 and 1973, Americans learned more and more about the facts behind the Watergate break-in. Several Nixon administration officials were found to have known about the planned burglary or to have helped conceal information about it afterward. The big question on everyone's mind was, Had the president known about it himself? Was he, too, part of the cover-up?

Nixon said he was not. But the evidence suggested he might be lying. If he was, there was a way to find out. The president was in the habit of secretly making tape recordings of conversations he had with his top aides in his White House office. In 1973, one of these aides disclosed that the president had tapes made just days after the break-in. If people could listen to those tapes, they might find out whether or not the president had known about the burglary and the cover-up conspiracy. They would also know more about just which Nixon aides and government officials had broken the law.

Government prosecutors who were trying to build court cases against those involved in Watergate were determined to get possession of the tapes. Nixon was just as determined to keep them to himself. He claimed that as chief executive, he had the privilege of deciding what evidence to give to the prosecutors and what to withhold.

So the prosecutors asked the courts to order Nixon to give up the tapes. Over the months, the case worked its way up through the judiciary. On July 8, 1974, Nixon's lawyer and a special Watergate prosecutor argued the matter orally before the Supreme Court.

The president's lawyer stressed his client's claim of executive privilege. A president is not subject to the law in the same way as the rest of us, he argued. "Law as to the President has to be applied in a constitutional way which is different than anyone else," he told the justices.

Would they agree? Or would they side with the special prosecutor? The prosecutor had a strong argument, too. "In refusing to produce the evidence . . . the President invokes the . . . Constitution," he said. "Now, the President may be right in how he reads the Constitution. But he may also be wrong. And if he is wrong, who is there to tell him so? And if there is no one, then the President, of course, is free to pursue his course of erroneous interpretations. What then becomes of our constitutional form of government?"

The justices listened attentively. It was a profound matter they were being asked to settle. Which was greater, the power of the president or the power of the law? The executive branch or the Constitution? How was the system of checks and balances to work in this case?

The country held its breath as it waited for the answers. One week went by. Then another.

On July 24, the suspense ended. The Court issued its ruling in *U.S.* v. *Nixon.* The president must surrender the tapes, the justices said. Their decision was a unanimous 8–0. Justice William Rehnquist, who had worked in the Nixon administration before coming onto the Court, did not participate in the case.

Once people heard the tapes they realized why Nixon had been so reluctant to give them up. The recordings made it clear that the president had known about the break-in from the start. He had been lying to the country for months. Within days, he announced his resignation.

As Nixon flew from Washington to his home in California, Vice-President Gerald R. Ford was sworn in as president. During his two and a half years in the White House, Ford named one man to the Court. This was Associate Justice John Paul Stevens. The next president, Democrat Jimmy Carter, did not get to nominate anyone to the Court. Carter, elected in 1976, ran for reelection four years later. He lost to Republican Ronald W. Reagan.

Reagan entered the White House eager to change the Court—and the country. During the campaign, he had made no secret of his ultraconservative philosophy. He favored judicial restraint and strict construction of the Constitution, and he condemned the recent Court decisions that had so altered American society.

Reagan's list of anti-Court grievances was a long one. He opposed affirmative action and the use of the courts to broaden minority rights. He disapproved of the Burger Court's decision in the *New York Times* censorship case, and he abhorred abortion. He supported prayer in public schools and detested the idea of busing to achieve racial integration. He claimed that Supreme Court rulings had made it difficult, if not impossible, for police forces to do their job of protecting the public. Like the Federalists of old, and like the laissez-faire Republicans of a later day, he placed the interests of business and industry over those of working men and women. And he was dedicated to building a Supreme Court that would share his ideas and put them to work in America.

Chief Justices

Earl Warren	1953-1969
Warren E. Burger	1969-1986

Associate Justices

John M. Harlan	1955-1971
William J. Brennan, Jr.	1956-
Charles E. Whittaker	1957-1962
Potter Stewart	1958-1981
Byron R. White	1962-
Arthur J. Goldberg	1962-1965
Abe Fortas	1965-1969
Thurgood Marshall	1967-
Harry A. Blackmun	1970-
Lewis F. Powell, Jr.	1972-
William H. Rehnquist	1972-
John P. Stevens	1975-

8

The Court in the Twenty-first Century

Ronald Reagan's first opportunity to change the Supreme Court came just five months after he took over as president. In June 1981, an associate justice resigned. To fill his place, the president appointed a judge of the Arizona State Court of Appeals.

The Arizona judge took the oath of office on September 25, 1981. For the one hundred first time since 1789, a new associate justice was swearing to "support and defend the Constitution of the United States of America." For the first time, a woman was doing it.

The oath-taking ceremony over, Associate Justice Sandra Day O'Connor stepped up to the bench. Proudly, she took the seat reserved for her at the end. By tradition, this spot belongs to the newest member of the Court. Justice O'Connor had joined "the brethren."

Reagan's first Court appointment seemed unlikely to be his last. By the time the president was reelected in 1984, five of the justices were aged seventy-five or more. At least one was in poor health. Three other justices were in their sixties. It looked as if the president would be naming three, four, or perhaps even five more justices before his second term of office expired.

The prospect dismayed many. If Reagan were to appoint several justices, chances were that all would be around

O'Connor's age—fifty-four in 1984. Each could be expected to remain on the Court for twenty or thirty years. That would mean Reagan might be picking a Supreme Court majority that would last a good two decades into the next century.

Is it right for one individual to have so much power for so long over the future of the nation's highest judicial body? Reagan's term of office was due to expire in 1989, yet his influence might be felt on the Court until the year 2020. As a second-term president, he would never again face American voters. The Twenty-Second Amendment to the Constitution, ratified in 1951, says no president may be elected to more than two full terms of office. Reagan could name whomever he liked to the Court without worrying that an unpopular choice might turn people against him in the next election.

Another concern was Reagan's extreme conservatism. Would he be handpicking an ultraconservative Court that would spend the first part of the twenty-first century trying to restore American society to what it had been in the 1940s and 1950s?

It seemed probable. Everyone knew the president's positions: for official government support of religion, the rights of the police, and the interests of business; against affirmative action and busing for integration. They knew he had vowed to appoint no federal court judge who did not personally oppose abortion. They could see that he was resolved to bring the country into line with his own particular moral and religious beliefs. They had heard one of his most enthusiastic backers, conservative Christian minister Jerry Falwell, assert that "we" will appoint between three and five new Supreme Court justices.

What did all this portend for the Court and for the country? Many thought it threatened to turn America, the land of "liberty and justice for all," into a place where the police and the courts dictate how people live their private lives; where members of minority groups are shut out of the social, political, and economic mainstream; and where the rich and strong flourish at the expense of the poor and powerless.

Others did not see the situation in the same light. Some, like Falwell, thoroughly approved of Reagan's plans for the

Court. Others simply did not believe that those plans would work out. No president can shape the Supreme Court for decades to come, they maintained.

Justice William Rehnquist said he felt this way. In a 1984 speech, Rehnquist asserted that presidents do not have the power to mold the Court. Presidents may think they are appointing justices who share their views and who will vote the way they want them to, but sometimes they find themselves surprised and disappointed. President Theodore Roosevelt named Oliver Wendell Holmes to the Court, believing Holmes would support his efforts to break up large corporations and make business practices fairer for all. Holmes did not. "I could carve out of a banana a judge with more backbone than that," Roosevelt complained. Fifty years later, President Eisenhower was shocked by Earl Warren's desegregation rulings.

Rehnquist might also have mentioned Eisenhower appointee William J. Brennan, Jr., who also turned out to be more liberal than the president may have expected. Brennan was still on the Court in 1985. Another appointee who disappointed the president who appointed him was Harry Blackmun. Named to the Court by antiabortionist Richard Nixon, he wrote the majority opinion in *Roe* v. *Wade,* the case that gave American women the legal right to terminate a pregnancy. Rehnquist could also have asked how Nixon must have felt when three of his nominees, Blackmun, Chief Justice Burger, and Lewis F. Powell, joined in ordering him to give up the Watergate tapes.

One point Rehnquist did emphasize was the security of a seat on the Court. Justices are appointed for life. Unless they indulge in serious misconduct, they cannot be removed from office. Only one justice, Samuel Chase, has been impeached, and he was not convicted. Thus, once a president's appointees are actually on the bench, they are safe, no matter what way they vote. The president does not control them, and he cannot tell them how to decide a case.

How valid were Rehnquist's points? He was the most conservative justice on the Court in 1985, the one in deepest sympathy with Reagan's views. Was this sympathy making him try

to calm Americans' apprehensions about possible Reagan nominees? Was this his method of paving the way for the country's acceptance of these nominees? A number of people were convinced it was.

Many also questioned Rehnquist's contention that Supreme Court appointees often turn away from the philosophy of those who put them on the bench in the first place. Some do, but most do not.

Rehnquist himself was as conservative in 1986 as he had been fourteen years earlier when he took his seat. Oliver Wendell Holmes opposed Theodore Roosevelt on one issue, but he backed the president fully on most others. Federalist John Adams was certainly pleased with John Marshall's leadership of the Court, and states' righter Andrew Jackson was pleased with Roger Taney's. President Ulysses Grant's two 1870 appointees did exactly what they were put on the Court to do. They voted to make paper money legal tender, reversing a decision made just the year before. President Franklin Roosevelt's appointments helped serve as a core for the very liberal Warren Court. Certainly, President Reagan must have been well satisfied with Justice O'Connor's numerous conservative opinions.

Beyond the question of whether or not a president can form a Supreme Court in his own image is the question of whether it is right even to try. Some, and Rehnquist is one of them, claim presidents do have such a right. Federalist presidents Washington and Adams availed themselves of that right. So did Republican Abraham Lincoln and Democrat Franklin Roosevelt, and no one is criticizing them. As the chart on page 92 shows, nearly half of the nation's presidents, nineteen out of forty, have named three or more Supreme Court justices. The only reason some people today worry about a Court majority appointed by Reagan is that they do not like Reagan's views of society and the role of government. They oppose a Reagan-appointed Court not on principle but for political reasons.

At least, that is the conservatives' view. Liberals respond that it is not they who are thinking in political terms. It is Reagan and his fellow conservatives themselves who are doing that.

The liberals agree that a president ordinarily picks Court nominees who agree with him in general terms. Republican presidents usually, though not always, choose Republican justices. Presidents who believe in judicial restraint select justices who also believe in judicial restraint. That is their privilege.

But, the liberals say, 1980s conservatives seek to go beyond general agreement with their ideas. They will be content with Court appointees who agree with them on precise and specific details. That is why they will not support any candidate for the federal judiciary who supports the Court's abortion decision in *Roe* v. *Wade*, for example. (The conservatives' antiabortion restriction applies to all federal judges, not just to Supreme Court appointees.) Many liberals are convinced that as new vacancies occurred on the Supreme Court, Reagan and his allies in the Senate would fill them only with men and women who shared their attitudes in other areas, too.

This could do more than ensure a conservative "Reagan Court" for the next thirty years. It could do to the Supreme Court what President Grant and the railroading interests in Congress did to it in 1870. The two new justices appointed and confirmed in that year were blatantly political choices. When the two voted in favor of paper money the next year, Americans reacted by expressing contempt for the Court and its decisions. If in the late 1980s, a conservative president and a conservative Senate were to succeed in creating a Court that obediently reverses decisions of which they disapprove, they, too, will have turned the Supreme Court into a political object. The Court's prestige will suffer.

In any case, the Supreme Court may become more conservative even without any narrowly political appointments. Early in 1985, most people agreed that the justices seemed to be moving in a conservative direction. Some thought the Court might be retreating from the liberalism of the 1960s and 1970s because its members knew they were being watched by a conservative president and a relatively conservative Congress. In 1985, the Republican party was in the majority in the

Senate, although Democrats held the House of Representatives. The threat that the president might persuade Congress to approve legislation that would overturn certain Court decisions was very real. Strong attempts to pass a constitutional amendment outlawing abortion had already been made in Congress.

Others believed the Court's apparent trend toward conservatism was the result of increasing conservatism in the country as a whole. It was, after all, the votes of millions of American men and women that had put Reagan in the White House and fifty-four Republicans in the hundred-member Senate. As columnist Finley Peter Dunne had observed in 1900, the Supreme Court follows the election returns.

Whatever its cause, the Burger Court's swing toward conservatism seemed clear as Reagan's second term began. One straw in the wind was the ruling in *New Jersey* v. *T.L.O.* T.L.O. was the Piscataway High School student accused of selling marijuana whom we met in Chapter 1.

The court found against T.L.O. in 1985. By a 6–3 vote, the justices cut back on students' Fourth Amendment rights, thereby increasing the powers of school officials and the police. Among those who voted with the majority were Nixon appointees Burger, Blackmun, Powell, and Rehnquist. Sandra O'Connor voted with them, and so did Kennedy appointee Byron R. White.

The same six made up the majority in another 1985 defendants' rights case. In *Oregon* v. *Elstad,* the court upheld the burglary conviction of an eighteen-year-old boy. The boy had confessed to the crime before being *"Miranda'ed"*—told of his rights, found constitutional in the 1966 case of *Miranda* v. *Arizona,* to remain silent and to be represented by a lawyer. After he finally was *Miranda'ed*, the boy again admitted to the theft. This second confession could be used to convict him, the six justices agreed. The three dissenters, Stevens, Marshall, and Brennan, criticized the decision in strong terms. The boy had only confessed the second time because he knew the police had heard him confess the first time, they said. If he had been properly informed of his constitutional rights, he might not have confessed at all. Brennan called the Court's decision "a potentially crippling blow to *Miranda* and the ability of the courts to safeguard the rights of persons accused of crimes."

Yet other decisions announced in 1985 made people wonder whether the Court really was growing so conservative after all. In the case of *Evitts* v. *Lucey*, for example, the justices ruled that convicted criminals have the right to effective legal representation when they appeal their cases. This was a step toward expanding defendants' rights, rather than limiting them. Another case, *Tennessee* v. *Garner*, established that the police may not shoot to kill a fleeing suspect who is neither armed nor dangerous.

In the matter of church-state relations, too, the Court's 1984–1985 term pleased most liberals and dismayed many conservatives. In four separate cases, the justices came down solidly against the kind of government sponsorship of religion that President Reagan and men like the Reverend Falwell advocated. *Wallace* v. *Jaffree* overturned an Alabama law that ordered public school students to observe a daily "moment of silence," a "moment" that Alabama state officials admitted was intended to be devoted to Christian prayer. In *Thornton* v. *Caldor*, the justices ruled that an employer may require a worker to be on the job on the particular day of the week that the worker observes as the Sabbath. And in two other cases, *Grand Rapids* v. *Ball* and *Aguilar* v. *Felton*, the Court decreed an end to programs under which public school funds are used to pay certain teachers in parochial schools.

What did the decision of this term add up to? Both liberals and conservatives found something to cheer about and something to condemn. The "quirky," "unpredictable" Burger Court certainly seemed to be living up to its reputation. Observers began to conclude that only as the present justices resigned and new ones took their places would the Court's direction become unmistakable. In the meantime, though, changes of a different kind might face the Court. Today, as always, there are those with suggestions for "improving" or "reforming" our highest judicial body.

Few of the suggestions are new. One that has been around since Thomas Jefferson's time is that of electing justices to fixed terms of office. Adopting this reform would make it impossible for a president to exert control over the Court for decades after he leaves the White House. That is one reason the idea appealed to many in 1985. Elected justices would be responsive to the current mood of the country, whatever that mood might be, say those who favor this reform.

Those who oppose it agree—and that is why they oppose it. Having an elected Court would make all three branches of government subject to the will of the people. It would mean complete majority rule, a dictatorship of the majority. Who then would protect the rights of the minority? Protecting the nation's minorities—racial, ethnic, religious, political, and cultural—has been one of the Supreme Court's great tasks. Sometimes the Court has risen to the task courageously; sometimes it has not. But an elected Court would find it difficult to defend a minority at all. As soon as a justice took an unpopular position he or she might be voted off the Court.

Another suggestion is to make the Court more "professional" by limiting membership to men and women who have served as lower court judges. Some who support this proposal point out that if it had been the rule in 1954, Earl Warren would never have headed the Court. Warren was a lawyer and had been attorney general of California as well as governor of the state, but he had never been a judge.

Critics of a judges-only requirement retort that if it had been the rule from the start, John Marshall would not have headed the Court, either. Nor would Roger Taney, Morrison Waite, or Charles Evans Hughes. Outstanding associate justices like Joseph Story, Louis Brandeis, and Felix Frankfurter would have been disqualified, too. With arguments like these on their side, the critics anticipated little difficulty in keeping a judges-only rule off the books.

But other changes may lie ahead for the Court. Chief Justice Burger had some in mind. One Burger suggestion was to create a new intermediate federal court of appeals. This court would be made up of judges from each of the nation's thirteen federal appeals courts. It would be sort of a "sub-Supreme Court." The court would meet once a year for four weeks. Its job would be hearing cases that involve conflicting rulings from the various federal appellate courts.

Burger was convinced that such a court is needed, just as a patent court was needed at the end of the last century. The modern Supreme Court is overworked, he claims. Thirty years ago, the justices heard fewer than 1500 cases a year. In 1984, 5100 were on the docket. "Years ago we passed any sensible limit on how much the Supreme Court should be asked to do," Burger told a meeting of American lawyers early in 1985. Each justice is entitled to hire four law clerks as assistants, but they must have even more help, Burger believed. The Chief Justice also wanted pay raises for Court members. In 1985, he was getting $104,700 a year. Associate judges were paid $100,600.

Warren Burger's second major suggestion was to increase the size of the Court by adding a tenth justice. The duties of this justice would be administrative, not judicial. He or she would act as and assistant to the Chief Justice, helping to manage the Court's affairs. It would be up to the Chief Justice to select the tenth, nonvoting member of the Court.

To critics, both of Burger's suggestions seem to fall outside the limits of the Constitution. That document allows Congress to set the size of the Court. It gives the president the right to choose its justices and the Senate the right to accept or reject those choices. It says nothing about the Chief Justice enlarging the Court or naming one of its members. Similarly, the Constitution refers to "one Supreme Court." It makes no mention of what Burger called an "intercircuit panel" to hear cases arising from contrary decisions by the federal appeals courts.

A third Burger suggestion was to give the Court more freedom to refuse cases. Under 1985 rules, the justices were forced to accept large numbers of rather similar cases. Each had to be considered and decided individually. New legislation is needed, Burger believed, to allow the justices to select only the most vital cases. Their decisions in those cases would then stand as precedents for others like them.

All eight of the Chief Justice's 1985 associates on the Court backed this last proposal. Bills to make it a reality were introduced in Congress every year between 1981 and 1984. Each time, a bill passed in one house but not in the other. Congress, it seemed, was reluctant to meddle with the Supreme Court.

No wonder. That Court has served the country well. It has had its bad times, of course, and its enemies. But it was the Supreme Court that welded thirteen bickering states together and made them the nucleus of one great nation. It was the Supreme Court that put the Constitution above all other law and made the system work. It was the Supreme Court that—finally—sought to breathe new life into the concept of liberty and equality for all.

What of the future? One great change came to the Court at the conclusion of its 1985-86 term. In June 1986 Warren Burger resigned from the Court, and President Reagan named William Rehnquist to succeed him as Chief Justice. To replace Rehnquist, the president appointed another conservative, Judge Antonin Scalia from the District of Columbia Court of Appeals.

So it was that under new leadership the Supreme Court approached its two hundredth birthday in 1990. As it enters its third century, many critical matters will come before it. Some will be new variations on the traditional issues of states' rights versus federal rights, individual rights versus the rights of government, minority rights versus the rights of the majority, and so forth.

Other cases will bring the Court into strange and difficult new areas, areas of modern science and technology. The justices will be deciding cases that arise out of disputes over ownership of new communications systems, the conflicting rights of industry and government in scientific research, the application of new medical techniques, and much more.

How will the Supreme Court go about resolving such complex issues? Cautiously, as the Taney Court so often did, or as the Burger Court frequently has? Conservatively, like a Fuller or a Taft Court? Or boldly, like a Marshall Court or a Warren Court? How will the Court of the twenty-first century measure up to the Courts of the past?

Chief Justice

William H. Rehnquist   1986-

Associate Justices

Sandra Day O'Connor   1981-
Antonin Scalia   1986-

Federal Judicial System

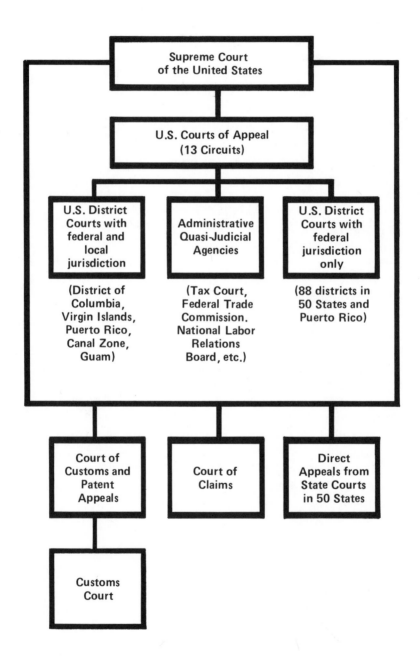

Supreme Court
of the United States

U.S. Courts of Appeal
(13 Circuits)

U.S. District
Courts with
federal and
local
jurisdiction

(District of
Columbia,
Virgin Islands,
Puerto Rico,
Canal Zone,
Guam)

Administrative
Quasi-Judicial
Agencies

(Tax Court,
Federal Trade
Commission.
National Labor
Relations
Board, etc.)

U.S. District
Courts with
federal
jurisdiction
only

(88 districts in
50 States and
Puerto Rico)

Court of
Customs and
Patent
Appeals

Court of
Claims

Direct
Appeals from
State Courts
in 50 States

Customs
Court

State Judicial System

```
┌─────────────────────────────────┐
│       State Supreme Court        │
└─────────────────────────────────┘
```

(Court of final resort. Some states call it Supreme Court, Supreme Court of Errors, Court of Appeals, Supreme Judicial Court, or Supreme Court of Appeals.)

```
┌─────────────────────────────────┐
│   Intermediate Appellate Courts  │
└─────────────────────────────────┘
```

(Only 20 of the 50 states have intermediate appellate courts, an intermediate appellate tribunal between the trial court and the court of final resort. A majority of cases are decided finally by the appellate courts.)

```
┌─────────────────────────────────┐
│      Trial Courts of Original and │
│         General Jurisdiction      │
└─────────────────────────────────┘
```

(Highest trial court with original and general jurisdiction. Some states refer to it as Circuit Court, District Court, Court of Common Pleas, and in New York, Supreme Court.)

```
┌─────────────────────────────────┐
│    Courts of Limited Jurisdiction │
└─────────────────────────────────┘
```

U.S. Supreme Court Justices

Name	Term	Appointed by

CHIEF JUSTICES

Name	Term	Appointed by
John Jay	1790-1795	Washington
John Rutledge	1795	†Washington
Oliver Ellsworth	1796-1800	Washington
John Marshall	1801-1835	J. Adams
Roger B. Taney	1836-1864	Jackson
Salmon P. Chase	1864-1873	Lincoln
Morrison R. Waite	1874-1888	Grant
Melville W. Fuller	1888-1910	Cleveland
Edward D. White	1910-1921	Taft
William H. Taft	1921-1930	Harding
Charles E. Hughes	1930-1941	Hoover
Harlan F. Stone	1941-1946	F. D. Roosevelt
Frederick M. Vinson	1946-1953	Truman
Earl Warren	1953-1969	Eisenhower
Warren E. Burger	1969-1986	Nixon
William H. Rehnquist	1986-	Reagan

ASSOCIATE JUSTICES

Name	Term	Appointed by
James Wilson	1789-1798	Washington
John Rutledge	1790-1791	Washington
William Cushing	1790-1810	Washington
John Blair	1790-1796	Washington
James Iredell	1790-1799	Washington
Thomas Johnson	1792-1793	Washington
William Paterson	1793-1806	Washington
Samuel Chase	1796-1811	Washington
Bushrod Washington	1799-1829	J. Adams
Alfred Moore	1800-1804	J. Adams
William Johnson	1804-1834	Jefferson
H. Brockholst Livingston	1807-1823	Jefferson
Thomas Todd	1807-1826	Jefferson
Gabriel Duvall	1811-1835	Madison
Joseph Story	1812-1845	Madison
Smith Thompson	1823-1843	Monroe
Robert Trimble	1826-1828	J.Q. Adams
John McLean	1830-1861	Jackson
Henry Baldwin	1830-1844	Jackson
James M. Wayne	1835-1867	Jackson
Philip P. Barbour	1836-1841	Jackson
John Catron	1837-1865	Van Buren
John McKinley	1838-1852	Van Buren
Peter V. Daniel	1842-1860	Van Buren
Samuel Nelson	1845-1872	Tyler
Levi Woodbury	1845-1851	Polk
Robert C. Grier	1846-1870	Polk
Benjamin R. Curtis	1851-1857	Fillmore
John A. Campbell	1853-1861	Pierce
Nathan Clifford	1858-1881	Buchanan
Noah H. Swayne	1862-1881	Lincoln
Samuel F. Miller	1862-1890	Lincoln
David Davis	1862-1877	Lincoln

† appointment not
confirmed by Senate

Stephen J. Field	1863-1897	Lincoln
William Strong	1870-1880	Grant
Joseph P. Bradley	1870-1892	Grant
Ward Hunt	1873-1882	Grant
John M. Harlan	1877-1911	Hayes
William B. Woods	1881-1887	Hayes
Stanley Matthews	1881-1889	Garfield
Horace Gray	1882-1902	Arthur
Samuel Blatchford	1882-1893	Arthur
Lucius Q. C. Lamar	1888-1893	Cleveland
David J. Brewer	1890-1910	Harrison
Henry B. Brown	1891-1906	Harrison
George Shiras, Jr.	1892-1903	Harrison
Howell E. Jackson	1893-1895	Harrison
Edward D. White	1894-1910	Cleveland
Rufus W. Peckham	1896-1909	Cleveland
Joseph McKenna	1898-1925	McKinley
Oliver W. Holmes, Jr.	1902-1932	T. Roosevelt
William R. Day	1903-1922	T. Roosevelt
William H. Moody	1906-1910	T. Roosevelt
Horace H. Lurton	1910-1914	Taft
Charles E. Hughes	1910-1916	Taft
Willis Van Devanter	1911-1937	Taft
Joseph R. Lamar	1911-1916	Taft
Mahlon Pitney	1912-1922	Taft
James C. McReynolds	1914-1941	Wilson
Louis D. Brandeis	1916-1939	Wilson
John H. Clarke	1916-1922	Wilson
George Sutherland	1922-1938	Harding
Pierce Butler	1923-1939	Harding
Edward T. Sanford	1923-1930	Harding
Harlan F. Stone	1925-1941	Coolidge
Owen J. Roberts	1930-1945	Hoover
Benjamin N. Cardozo	1932-1938	Hoover
Hugo L. Black	1937-1971	F.D. Roosevelt
Stanley F. Reed	1938-1957	F.D. Roosevelt
Felix Frankfurter	1939-1962	F.D. Roosevelt
William O. Douglas	1939-1975	F.D. Roosevelt
Frank Murphy	1940-1949	F.D. Roosevelt
James F. Byrnes	1941-1942	F.D. Roosevelt
Robert H. Jackson	1941-1954	F.D. Roosevelt
Wiley B. Rutledge	1943-1949	F.D. Roosevelt
Harold H. Burton	1945-1958	Truman
Tom C. Clark	1949-1967	Truman
Sherman Minton	1949-1956	Truman
John M. Harlan	1955-1971	Eisenhower
William J. Brennan, Jr.	1956-	Eisenhower
Charles E. Whittaker	1957-1962	Eisenhower
Potter Stewart	1958-1981	Eisenhower
Byron R. White	1962-	Kennedy
Arthur J. Goldberg	1962-1965	Kennedy
Abe Fortas	1965-1969	Johnson
Thurgood Marshall	1967-	Johnson
Harry A. Blackmun	1970-	Nixon
Lewis F. Powell, Jr.	1972-	Nixon
William H. Rehnquist	1972-	Nixon
John P. Stevens	1975-	Ford
Sandra Day O'Connor	1981-	Reagan
Antonin Scalia	1986-	Reagan

Further Reading

BOOKS

Asch, Sidney H. *The Supreme Court and Its Great Justices.* New York: Arco, 1971.

Murphy, Walter F. *Congress and the Court.* Chicago: University of Chicago Press, 1962.

Steamer, Robert J. *The Supreme Court in Crisis: A History of Conflict.* Amherst: University of Massachusetts Press 1971.

Witt, Elder, ed. *The Supreme Court: Justice and the Law,* 2nd edition. Washington, D.C.: Congressional Quarterly, Inc., 1977.

PERIODICALS

Greenhouse, Linda. "Burger Urges Congress To Help Cut Court Load." *The New York Times,* December 31, 1984.

_____. "Court Backs Prosecution on Confession Issue in Miranda Rule." *The New York Times*, March 5, 1985.

_____. "High Court Upsets Alabama Statute on School Prayer." *The New York Times*, June 5, 1985.

_____. "High Court Voids Connecticut Sabbath Law." *The New York Times*, June 27, 1985.

_____. "Justices Uphold Student Searches When Reasonable." *The New York Times*, January 16, 1985.

Jenkins, John A. "The Partisan: A Talk With Justice Rehnquist." *The New York Times Magazine*, March 3, 1985.

Kaufman, Irving R. "Keeping Politics Out of the Court." *The New York Times Magazine*, December 9, 1984.

Podesta, Anthony T. "Court-Packing, Reagan-Style." *The New York Times*, July 26, 1985.

Taylor, Stuart Jr. "Justice Stevens, in Rare Criticism, Disputes Meese on Constitution." *The New York Times*, October 26, 1985.

Thomas, Evan. "Court at the Crossroads." *Time*, Vol. 124, No. 15, October 8, 1984.

Index